Nick,

Thank you

for bringing Tossed [F]
to life °

Sarah

Diva hugo !

Tossed & Found

...Where Frugal *is* Chic

Barb Tobias

Diva
Press

Tossed & Found…Where Frugal is Chic
by Barb Tobias

Published by Mile High Press in collaboration with Diva Press

mile high press

Diva Press

Cover and Interior Design: NZ Graphics
Editor: John Maling

Library of Congress Catalog Control Number: 2010931850

ISBN: 978-1-885331-35-9

1) Thrift Shopping 2) Garage Sales 3) Frugal Living 4) Recycling
5) Women's Self-help 6) Green Living

First Edition Printed in Canada

Books may be purchased by contacting the publisher at:
BarbTobias@ThriftTalkDiva.com
Website: www.ThriftTalkDiva.com

Table of Contents

Acknowledgements

To my amazing and supportive Diva-pals who read each mistake ridden edition of this book, and continued to continue.

To my amazing book shepherds, Dr. Judith Briles and Katherine Carol, who kept such vigilant watch over this aspiring writer and mistress-fully led her into authorship.

To John Maling who edited with a gentle but finely honed blade.

To Nick Zelinger who's graphic artistry captured the Diva spirit and brought her to life from cover to copy.

To Scott who inadvertently led me into the vortex of my storm … and new beginnings.

To Stephen who made it all possible.

And finally to providence; riding high on the wings of change, determined to relentlessly dog me … and, forever empower me.

Dedication

To all those that have found themselves tossed about.
And with humble affection … to those feisty souls
who found themselves again.

Introduction

My lust for tarnished treasure, coupled with the sheer thrill of the hunt, became an obsession that held me tight within its steely grip. I was fascinated with Bargain America and succumbed to its relentless, beckoning finger, its promise of secondhand booty ... and a better life.

Over time, and despite the occasional rip-off or bargain blooper, my homes became living testaments to the fabulous riches I uncovered. The enterprising thrift venues and motley garages that hawked their sordid wares enthralled me, capturing my attention and every spare moment.

The many resourceful, veteran thrifters who shared their secrets also taught me the art of uncovering the unusual. These warriors became my teachers and steadfast comrades; wise and frugal sages who cheerfully sloughed off the stigma of hunting for used goods in exchange for the triumphs of discovering once-in-a-lifetime finds.

On the other side of the street, my conventional friends not only tolerated my thrift-aholic tendencies, but observed with voyeuristic glee the transformation of my humble abodes into richly appointed dwellings. With loving encouragement, they relentlessly dogged me to turn my love affair with thrift into the book you are holding ... an addictive, inspiring and often playful journey that walks the reader through my personal hardships and triumphant successes.

Each chapter begins with a pictorial memory; a glimpse of my transformation from farm girl—to fashion model—to self-proclaimed thrift Diva.

My passage was not easy. Each step I took along the way was fraught with indecision, and I reacted to each experience like a gate swinging in a storm; vacillating between inspiration and rejection, shrinking and blossoming.

Tossed & Found is more than a thrifting adventure, or a "how-to" outlining the rescue of *rejects* tossed aside by uncaring hands. Each page I wrote served as a cathartic release; a reflection of the many times I felt *tossed* around by the relentless waves that crashed against the shores of my life.

Stroll with me, in my self-appointed Diva-ness, as we explore a newly frugal nation, and I share the tricks of selling, the art of bargaining and the thrill of buying other people's junk.

Tossed

My former life vanished … gone … kaput! I was on my own, raising a son … and fraught with the challenges of starting over. To add salt to my wounds, frugality and restraint were not hands I was used to playing.

It took being tossed out on my proverbial bum to teach me how to budget, recycle and shop the tattered thrift venues that peppered my town. Hesitantly, I dipped my toes into the murky waters of what I viewed as a distasteful pool of hand-me-downs and rejects. Little did I know that I would soon be haunting those humble pinnacles of second-hand goods; that the hunt would become my obsession … and ultimately my liberation.

Thrifty Something

Alone and frightened, I entered my "thrifties" fighting to live stylishly on an ever-diminishing budget. Moreover, it simply wasn't chic during that affluent era to buy clothes or household items from garage sales or thrift stores.

I am a Boomer. My generation saw unprecedented prosperity, and believed that material comforts and social status were our birthrights. And I, like my contemporaries, was seduced by slick adverting that tempted me with luxurious lifestyles, replete with designer labels, bigger homes, racier cars, foreign vacations, and even more exotic pets.

Although I yearned to wear fashionable clothes and live in stunning homes, I knew

I had to control my spending. But, I wasn't hardwired to clip coupons, nor was I inclined to adhere to the money-saving regimens touted by so many of the frugal fashionistas of the time.

I needed to find a cheap alternative that would satiate my creative desires and resonate with me at a core level; a frugal quest that would be fun and enticing.

Then … I happened upon a garage sale.

The Turning Point

The details of that first sale are not only inked in my memory, but that event turned out to be a pivotal point in my tumultuous life. The fact that I even went to a tag sale evidenced my wobbly financial state.

It wasn't a planned event; I simply noticed a lowly garage sale sign at the side of the road, mocking me, prophetically luring me in with the promise of amusement and perhaps a found treasure or two.

As I pulled up to my target, I realized with an incredulous shake of my head that I was feeling uncomfortable. Nervous.

This was insane.

I was a fashion model for God's sake. This thing I was about to do, partaking in some back-alley shenanigans, just felt creepy.

If the truth be known, I was broke. Long gone were the heady days of shopping at Saks Fifth Avenue and the trendy designer boutiques. Disheartened and dispirited, I bemoaned the fact that lately there was always more month than money.

I had promised myself, ad nauseam, that I wouldn't look back to those carefree and revenue rich days. But like the reaper steals into the night, the perceived injustice of my plight bore down on me with oppressive might. Sitting in my car looking deep into a stranger's dank and dusky garage, I was overcome with a heavy sense of hopelessness. It was overwhelming. I tried to ignore the tear that left its trace through my makeup. I was miserable.

How had I ended up even considering shopping at someone else's junk-strewn sale?

"Pull yourself together," I hissed at the reflection in my rearview mirror. "This isn't a media interview; it's a garage sale; just a little test—a life lesson."

Momentarily bolstered by my fleeting warrior persona, I reprimanded myself and jockeyed my disreputable car into position between a decrepit trailer and an enormous van, parked across the road from the sale.

I remained in the safety of my car longer than I needed, collecting my thoughts while repairing my makeup. Reaching for my sunglasses and floppy hat, I realized that I was still dawdling, while my old tin-can of a car grew increasingly hot.

Cutting myself a little slack, I labored to convince myself that this could be fun despite the fact that I had always viewed thrifting as a fairly seedy affair brimming with used stuff—unwanted, dirty and most likely … smelly. Yuck.

Another thought flicked through my mind stopping me momentarily, "What about garage sale etiquette?" I fretted over this question. Admittedly, I was totally ignorant of what the shopping protocol was, or if there even was such a thing. I didn't know how to act. I had no clue as to what to do, say, or offer.

Garage sale etiquette, schmetiquette, where is the bling?

Retail shopping I got; I would simply survey new merchandise, make my selections, try them on in a well lit, comfortable dressing room, hand them to the nice sales lady, pay the sticker price and leave

… with new, tissue wrapped treasures. Neat. Easy. Familiar. And … costly.

The Procrastinator

Shifting my legs from one sticky spot to a dryer, hotter section of my beat-up leather seat, I realized that I was seriously procrastinating.

A movie trailer moment flashed through my mind, recalling the times my sister eagerly showed me the wonderful finds she had collected during her many thrifting jaunts. I didn't mask my distain, and I still cringe at my haughty reaction to her gleeful excitement over discovering and purchasing someone else's junk.

"Well, times have definitely changed." I sighed in resignation.

Wincing at the biting blast of heat that hit me when I opened the car door, I hesitantly stepped onto the sweltering pavement and walked up the driveway toward my future.

So call me spoiled … if garage sales don't have dressing rooms, count me out!

Tarnished

Strewn about the yard, littering the driveway and piled on tables and benches throughout the sale were heaps of unmarked castoffs. Each leaned or sat in varying states of haphazard display, cooking in the relentless heat.

At this point, far more than any interest in pursuing the dismal hand-me-downs petitioning for a new home, I sought release from the burning sun in the refuge of the dank but significantly cooler garage. Relief.

Once my eyes adjusted to the dim interior, I spotted a rather young gal sitting at a card table in the back recesses of her pitiful cavern. She was listlessly arranging bits and pieces of costume jewelry on a stand, refusing to raise her head in acknowledgement of my arrival.

A quick scan of the crude interior held nothing to pique my interest. I was preparing to leave when I spotted an ornate and deeply tarnished butter server with a tall, elaborate, flip-back top peeking from behind an assortment of dusty and varied glassware. Reaching through the precarious assortment of grimy bottles blocking its view, I pulled the piece out. I felt a tingle and smiled at the heft of its telltale weight. Monitoring my rising excitement, I checked to see if the glass dish was still nestled safely within. Yes, there it was.

Acting nonchalant, on the outside chance that I was being watched, I casually turned the piece over to look for the revealing silver mark that would confirm its worth. It too was there.

"*I have to have this piece.*" I thought, quickly assessing my meager budget.

I turned toward the solitary proprietor who still, it seemed, had not noticed me. Her hair covered her face, blocking me from view. She looked busy, and was now ferociously shoving masses of used and wrinkled plastic bags into a box next to her checkout station.

"Excuse me," I offered apologetically, hesitant to disrupt her stoic concentration for fear of offending her before I could claim my prize.

"How much is this old butter dish?" I ventured. She looked up and eyed the item dispassionately. Turning away she continued stuffing the box, mumbling something about having to deal with her grandmother's old stuff.

For a moment I thought she might not answer me, or she was calculating how much she should charge me.

Finally in a voice full of resignation, or disinterest, I didn't know which, she shrugged, "Oh, whatever, how about five dollars?"

Stunned, and almost dropping the dish, I raced to whip out the cash, terrified that she might reconsider the value of the piece and change her mind.

Although I had no garage sale experience, I knew instinctively that this piece was a worthy find.

"There you go." I said as I paid her. "Ah, I think I'll look around just a bit longer."

Before I knew it I was rummaging through her boxes and piles of paraphernalia like a pro, dropping all vestiges of propriety and decorum. I removed my sunglasses. So much for dignity … I was having a ball.

Destiny met me in the back of a dimly lit garage, amidst the clutter and muddle of secondhand possibilities.

Burrowing through an assortment of dusty boxes I spied a fabulous, aging print of an elegant woman dressed in costume. I imagined that she was attending a masquerade ball set somewhere in the late 1800s. It was displayed in a beautiful but battered frame, and I knew I had to have this piece as well. Praying that my fortunes would hold, I asked again, "And what do you want for this old print?"

"Oh," she responded "That was my grandmother's too. It's been hanging around in this garage for years. I'll take five bucks as well."

Fearing she might reaccess its value, I quickly paid the five dollars, warily thanking her while making a fast exit, protectively cradling my precious cargo in my arms.

At this juncture I was oblivious to the oppressive heat that assaulted me as I opened the car door and tucked my trophies behind my seat.

Braving stifling temperatures, in the middle of nowhere, I knew I had found my niche ... my passion.

There was only one thing racing through my mind ... I had to find the next sale!

A Welcomed Obsession

As time went on, it was obvious that the incessant tides that pushed their tarnished chests of second-hand booty towards me were also carrying me into my frugal future. To resist the tempting lure of their possibilities was beyond my comprehension or desire.

Although I relished my new found obsession, I was still too proud to admit to my friends that I was a regular patron of the natty salvage dens scattered throughout town. I dreaded the inevitable moment I would meet someone I knew while digging through a box of kitchen utensils at some motley yard sale.

I became defensive about attending these sales even though I was unquestionably "in the zone" whenever I was sifting through someone's old castaways. My pride taunted me incessantly, harshly, reminding me that *Aspiring Divas simply do not thrift!*

Slowly, things began to look up. I was making my living as a fashion model, had just opened my own dog training school and was doing a fair share of radio and television appearances. In defense of my hesitancy to disclose my frugal passion, I would cringe at the thought of my public catching me red-handed; buried shoulder deep burrowing through a storage bin in the back of some grimy shed.

Image was paramount to me back then. I bowed to my ego whenever propriety reared her arrogant head. She shamed me into squashing a floppy hat onto my blonde tresses and pushing a pair of sunglasses on my haughty nose before I set out to explore the land of "Castoffs and Booty." After all, I had a fragile public image to protect!

Remembering those early, heady days of clandestine bargain hunting, I laugh at the lengths I went to … just to avoid discovery. Whenever I saw someone I knew, I would slink behind a garage, or move to the backside of a convenient hutch or scoot to the far side of an overloaded clothes rack … just to evade the supposed enemy.

My ridiculous antics and attempts to avoid those that I recognized were beyond arrogance and, in retrospect, pretty pathetic.

On occasion I would be recognized and forced into an uncomfortable conversation. Embarrassed, I would blurt out some absurd excuse to justify my presence at the sale rather than admitting that I was simply a helpless victim of my own compulsions.

A word to the wise: never wear stiletto heels when thrift shopping. They're a dead give-a-way.

Prophetically, these chance encounters taught me that people from all walks of life actually shopped thrift. Some penny-wise shoppers patronized them for financial reasons, as did I, while other aficionados simply loved the thrill of the hunt … as did I.

Even though I continued to wrestle with my pompous demons, they were never strong enough to stop me from pursuing the hidden potential within the ranks of the lively garage sales and dusty thrift shops.

Becoming a Regular

Immersing myself in the quest for gently used items, I discovered that thrift stores offered amazing deals. And, thankfully, they also kept regular store hours. Not only did I shop at these economical establishments during the off-season, but I began to frequent them whenever they held their sales; regularly scheduled days that offered 50 to 75 percent off.

It wasn't long before I became a "regular" on the circuit, picking up the art of bargaining, quibbling and wrangling from the *professionals*; those wise sages of sift and thrift that had been shopping the bargain venues for years. Each contributed to my knowledge and graciously taught me the difference between antique and vintage, and the advantages of patronizing estate sales versus garage sales.

Mercy, did someone use the term REGULAR? Need I remind everyone that this Diva doesn't have a "regular" bone in her fabulous body!

As week wound into weekend I could be found stationed at my computer painstakingly charting every tempting sale within an hour's drive, and breaking my list into Friday, Saturday and Sunday excursions.

Armed with maps and my priceless information bank of thrift sale descriptions, I knew that I was bound to run into my share of loser events. But by sheer numbers, I also knew I would come across some great bargains and score some grand finds.

I became a student, studying the art of thrifting by emulating the street-smart veterans I befriended. I learned where each bountiful flea market staked its claim, which days charitable stores ran their sales and when the professionals running estate sales were ready to bargain.

Be flexible: Hunting for thrift calls for one to embrace the unknown . . . and the unexpected.

A Collector of Orphans

I became the queen of the unwanted; a collector of "orphans." I snatched up the rejects that others passed over, and affectionately embraced the blemished, the bruised and the scarred.

Like metal to magnets, yard sales and thrift stores pulled me into their murky depths and dimly lit recesses.

Spotting décor that was unique or unusual soon became my specialty … my signature talent. I was routinely drawn to items that were dramatic, had great style and demanded attention.

My attraction to over-the-top décor pieces was insatiable and my home began to take on a museum-like quality; a portent of the brewing storm.

Ignoring the obvious, flawed objects took on a new light as my creative eye matured. The hidden potential beneath the decaying layers of tarnish or grime began to surface more quickly as my skills and artistry grew.

I learned to fix broken legs, repair antique frames, and mend holes in worn out throws. I discovered that items with peeling paint could be transformed with a simple sanding followed by a tasteful coat of color.

OK, so I have a little flair for the dramatic; a little bling, a little caviar, a little Porsche . . . Get over it!

Oil stains became my closest friends, and I began to turn the scratched and marred into things of beauty. I learned which products took off rust, what transformed mirrors into bright reflectors, and which oils worked on thirsty furniture.

Whenever I thought a piece worthy of purchase, I would first consider its assets by turning it one way, then another. "What can I do with you? How would you look in a different color? What would it cost me to repair you?"

Once I made the decision to rescue a waif, I would purchase the item if I felt that its condition warranted the price. Otherwise, I would make a reasonable offer hoping for acceptance or at least a friendly haggle.

After awhile I began to get a sense for which sellers were anxious to unload their 'white elephants' and which were going to be sticklers. Depending on how much I wanted the piece, I would make an offer, or counter ... or not.

❧

A bargain ain't a bargain unless it's something you need.
~ Sidney Carroll, *A Big Hand for the Little Lady*

❧

Transformation

The cleaning and rejuvenation practice began as soon as I lugged my "strays" home. I enjoyed restoring worn things almost as much as I delighted in the hunt.

The last time I rescued a stray he ate me out of house and home …

This phase was magical. My inner artistry was ignited. Scrutinizing my treasure's every detail, I studied its features, scars and lines. The fine qualities were lovingly considered and its objectionable traits measured. I took time with my new possessions while deciding how to utilize them … how to bring them alive.

During this thought provoking time, my resourceful nature was repeatedly challenged. Repurposing took a lot of thought and creativity. Items were repeatedly moved from one location to another in order to view them in a different light.

I'm fanatical about using tired pieces in unusual ways and often relegate furnture to rooms far different from their original intent.

An antique dresser might find its way into a den surrounded by Indian artifacts; a bedroom throw could be found tossed across a chair in a dining room to use on cool evenings; a family room armoire might make the perfect linen closet.

Paint was a consideration for some pieces, while oil stains became the coating of choice for the more salvageable items. On occasion, a complete stripping and refinishing was necessary for deeply damaged mongrels.

On the other hand, I began to value the homey appeal of *shabby chic*, appreciating its worn but distinctive charm … its flaws and character lines. On occasion, I would decide that the best action was no action at all—leaving a disfigured piece intact—a testament to its lofty service.

Chapter 2

... And
FOUND

Two more decades passed; years in which I lived fully, loved with abandon and lost irretrievably. I was beginning to feel the sun on my face as I entered my fortieth year, and was shedding my awkward skin, layer by layer.

Rising from the ashes of my chaos, a warrior spirit began to emerge. A light flickered in my darkness; a surprising and humble beacon that revealed my love affair with thrift.

I was growing stronger. The years of social unknowing were waning. The effortlessness of borrowed wealth and the despair over financial disaster were fading into the past. I had picked myself up from a failed marriage and charged, head down, into resolute singleness.

Regardless of my growing spirit, I still felt compelled to hide my parsimonious passion, changing my identity whenever I thrifted. My oversized dark glasses and floppy hat were constant companions.

The Seduction of a Generation

On the outside, times were changing as well. Back-alley thrifting was starting to make its move onto Main Street, determined to stand front and center. Resale shopping, utilizing secondhand products and conscious waste management were coming into vogue. The early apologetic days were over. Thrifting had become a smart and environmentally responsible way of life.

Be thrifty, but not covetous.
~George Herbert

Whether the swing was due to the downward spiral of the economy or to a nation answering the call to live consciously, Americans began to see the wisdom in buying recycled goods. Thrift shops began to boom, and garage and yard sales became not only a social Mecca but also a clearing center for the nation's clutter.

And I, along with the thrift world, had grown into my Diva shoes. Admittedly, it took me a while to get over myself and shed my covert antics and shame over my frugal shopping sprees.

My hobby was finding acceptance within the ranks of the masses, and I had found a voice. I became a mentor for those seeking to go green; a dicey Diva for those in quest of fashionably frugal decorations for their homes and bodies. Finally.

It was comforting to learn that I was no longer alone in my pursuit of secondhand possessions. Multitudes of thrifty shoppers were clambering aboard the thrift bandwagon. Frugal venues were packed while the fashionable malls were experiencing record dips in numbers.

Thrift had grown up.

Today, the industry is thriving. It is hard to tell whether the shift was due to enlightenment or resignation. Only time will tell. These days, people are simply more amenable to buying used goods despite the fact that they camouflage their second-hand purchases with euphemisms like *slightly tarnished, gently-used, recycled* or *green*.

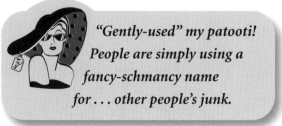

"Gently-used" my patooti! People are simply using a fancy-schmancy name for . . . other people's junk.

Chapter 3

Be Prepared

B*e prepared! Be prepared!* That's the Boy Scouts solemn creed. How many times had I heard, recited, and memorized that rite of passage for the All-American boy?

Growing up with two brothers, the oldest of which became an Eagle Scout, I can still recite all his scout codes ... verbatim.

I believe, more so now than then, that the most important trait for aspiring thrift addicts is to be prepared, organized, and equipped. Little did I realize that a childhood task would ready me for my life as a thrift-aholic.

Scouting

John, the eldest of my three siblings, memorized every creed, honor code and doctrine from the Cub Scout's Webelo ranks to the lofty Eagle Scouts. Every inch of his honor sash was covered with tidy round merit awards. Before each Scout meeting, it took a herculean effort to adjust this tribute to his pride-filled chest.

Standing second in line to the sibling watering hole, I was in awe of John's scouting accomplishments, and willingly assumed the role of his coach and prompter. Quizzing him faithfully on the key elements of the Webelo, Bobcat, Tiger, Wolf and Bear handbooks, he and I, in tandem, became adroit scouts, he in the limelight, and me in the wings.

As the years passed, John continued to add additional symbols of achievement to his uniform, having duly studied and passed each tier. The fallout from those nightly drills, resulted in my knowing every section of the Scout manuals ... better than he did; giving weight to the claim that the best way to learn something is to teach it.

True Grit

On the other hand, my organization of choice was our local 4-H club. Not that it was much of a choice; I simply followed my girlfriends into the ranks of the many country kids who played farmer.

What does one call a female farmer? A farmess?

The social aspects of the meetings were scary for me as I was painfully shy. I don't remember gaining any great life lessons from them, but I do remember the 4-H pledge. By then, I was really good at memorizing … anything.

I pledge my Head to clearer thinking, my Heart to greater loyalty, my Hands to larger service, and my Health to better living, for my club, my community, and my country.

I didn't have a sibling mentor prompting me during my memorization rituals … turnabout didn't seem to be in the cards. But then, it really didn't matter. Rather than achieving a sought-after rank, my focus turned to winning blue ribbons for my yummy brownies (which I never won), and flaunting my hand sewn aprons (which I never wore) to everyone who stopped by the farm.

The Diva Code

Memorizing those scout honor codes continued to influence me as I walked up the steps of life, so much so that it occurred to me that the thrift industry should have an honor code as well.

I understand. You are probably shaking your head and muttering, *Puleeeze*, right about now. But, bear with me.

Shopping is essential to our lives and is an integral part of every household in the world. (Okay, so for many of us female types, it is also

seriously enjoyable.) It is important to our lifestyles and finances. And, few receive the credit due when savvy and prudent shopping practices are carried out.

The shopping process involves many complex elements: shoppers need to be organized; find the best deals; bargain effectively; avoid purchasing mistakes and be willing and able to return things that do not work.

Now there's a humdinger ... Be Poised to Purchase!

Therefore, I believed that the thrifters of America needed a motto, just like the Boy Scouts. So I made one up ... *Be Poised to Purchase.* HA! Perfect!

Sure, that motto might be a bit cheeky, but there is truth behind my jest. When we thrift we need to be ready, prepared ... our cars, our work spaces, our homes. Organization reduces chaos, manages time, cleans up environments and can even prevent random buying impulses.

At this juncture in my life, I need very little. But, I still love to shop. I adore a bargain. And, I enjoy transforming raggedy discoveries into treasures.

However, I shop differently now. During my early frenzied days, thrift was a novel idea, and the thought of leaving a super bargain on the table drove me to distraction.

Today I am patient, realizing that the bargain coffers are always full. And, I really have everything I *need* . . . simply not everything I *want.* Big difference.

My shopping attitude has become refined over time. I now view "cheap" in a whole new light.

I know where to shop, how to bargain and the value of most things. Now I limit my thrift purchases to major sale days, shopping during 99¢ offers, or whenever the thrift venues offer huge discounts.

Today my shopping excursions are limited to the last day of tag or estate sales when merchandise is offered at 50 percent to 75 percent off . . . even, in some cases, given away freely.

The bottom line is, if I can't buy my merchandise for pennies on the dollar, I simply don't buy.

Experience has taught me to be ready for all sorts of challenges when buying, transporting and refurbishing secondhand goods. In other words, I am always *Poised to Purchase!*

Chapter 4

The Thriftmobile

M y car is my office. More specifically, my car could be considered my desk, and the stuff I carry around in it—my equipment.

Like most Americans, I bought my cars for their looks, performance, color and comfort. Today my transportation choices are determined by the amount of cargo they hold!

Landsakes! What Diva worth her salt would choose cargo room over driving a snazzy little sports car?

Time, energy and gas are wasted if I am forced to make multiple trips to pick up items that I had to leave behind because I couldn't fit them in my vehicle.

Over the years I have whittled my transportation needs down to:

1. a car that runs reliably;
2. has super storage bragging rights;
3. and sports a sturdy rooftop carrier.

My penchant for big, over-the-top furniture and decorative pieces is legendary. Therefore, I often need help hoisting or maneuvering gargantuan loads inside or onto the top of my car. I've learned to ask for a hand whenever faced with such daunting tasks. As a matter of fact, I now make it part of the deal.

Of course, I always ask in a friendly, half-kidding manner, but I am deadly serious. And I've never been turned down.

People have enlisted their teens, neighbors and friends to help load and unload all sorts of things. When wanting to get rid of their stuff, they will find some way or someone to help pack and load.

Believe me, over time, these acts of mercy have saved my Diva back and dignity.

When shopping for thrift, be flexible; embrace the unknown . . . value the unexpected.

The List

I carry a supply of essentials in my car for breaking down large pieces, or to assist with packing, loading or unloading:

- **Rope**: Two 25-foot lengths of strong rope come in handy when securing large items within or on top of the car.
- **Blankets:** A thriftmobile should stock several large blankets and three to four smaller ones to use as padding.
- **Clean rags:** A good supply of clean rags comes in handy when cleaning up spills or wiping down dirty items before placing them in the car.
- **Plastic ties:** These great bundlers have a million uses: binding loose items, securing latches, and even holding a flopping tailgate together. The list is endless.
- **Sanitizing wipes:** These indispensable cloths are perfect for quick cleanups.
- **Large plastic bags:** Spread across seats or on floors, these impenetrable dirt fighters keep a vehicle free from the grunge that accumulates when grimy treasures are tossed inside. Diva Tip: They also double as a nifty emergency raincoat.

The only ties I admire are the snappy bowties on those big handsome dudes at all the chic soirees I attend!

- **Five or six carpet remnants:** Rugs are handy aids that can be thrown between fragile objects or stacked items.
- **Nail repair kit:** (Just kidding!)
- **Various-length bungees:** A dozen or so of these expandable fasteners work well when binding objects of all sizes.
  (Note: Use only the metal hooked bungees as you will find that the plastic-tipped varieties break easily.)
- **Toolbox:** A set of small tools is necessary for repairing items on the spot or breaking down large pieces of furniture.

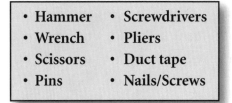

- Hammer   • Screwdrivers
- Wrench   • Pliers
- Scissors • Duct tape
- Pins   • Nails/Screws

Poised to Purchase

One weekend I was caught unprepared while shopping with a girlfriend at a local garage sale. Jo was new to the thrift scene, and as chance would have it she spied a great chair that we both thought was an excellent buy. Fitting it into her car however, was a different matter.

No matter how we twisted or angled it, we could not squeeze it into her vehicle. Frustrated, we eventually decided to leave the chair hanging out the back hatch, secured with a series of ropes and bungees.

As a newbie, Jo was not prepared for hauling furniture, while I, on the other hand, was pretty darn proud of my well-equipped vehicle. Luckily we had each driven a vehicle. With a fair degree of Diva flourish, I smugly announced that I had everything we needed and that we would be off and running in a jiffy.

I walked confidently to my vehicle to get my bungees, only to find that they were not in their normal spot.

After another futile search, we spotted a repairman working across the street.

Humbled by desperation, we meekly sought his help. Using a bit of femme fatale diplomacy, we asked whether he had some rope we might use to secure our chair.

True to the heroic spirit of repairmen the world over, he not only produced a length of rope, he also moved things around,

Hey there, big fella! If you're not doing anything at the moment, do you think you could help this little old Diva out and hoist this refrigerator onto the top of my car?

repositioned the chair and secured the hatch for us. This gallant gentleman proved again that people (particularly nice, husky guys) are generous and helpful when it comes to rescuing Divas in distress. We thanked him profusely as we drove off, celebrating our firmly lashed treasure.

Don't Leave Home Without It

There are five other essentials that are crucial to a successful day of Diva thrift shopping:

- **Garage sale map.** The night before my thrifting excursions, I make a map (from the Internet) of every garage sale and estate sale that I intend to hit. These detailed maps display the address and directions for each sale. My preferred mapping sites are: www.gsalr.com and www.EstateSales.net.
- **Voice recorder.** Early on, and deep in the throes of a thrifting adventure, I would jot down my thoughts as I was driving … yikes! Then I got smart. A mini tape recorder now captures reminders, street names, and addresses.

- **GPS.** I am serious about the thrift game and I don't want to waste time finding tricky locations. I program every address into my GPS and go from one house to another without a hitch.

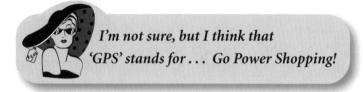

I'm not sure, but I think that 'GPS' stands for . . . Go Power Shopping!

- **Emergency Makeup Kit.** Every Diva needs to look her best after an afternoon of digging in grimy bins looking for an abandoned treasure.
- **Cash.** Need I explain? Just never leave home without it.

From Road-Kill ...

Chapter 5

to Road-Thrill

When road-kill beckons, the hunters become the hunted! Abandoned furniture and discarded possessions prey on unsuspecting travelers. They bide their time. They wait. Hovering, they anticipate the perfect moment to reveal themselves, luring their victims into their snares with the promise of yet another trophy.

These road-shoulder diversions materialize at the worst possible moments. They detain tardy passersby, resplendent in their fancy frugality, intent on arriving at their appointments intact.

However, these harried treasure seekers are rendered helpless under such alluring seduction ... and inevitably, they succumb.

A Tempting Summons

Roadside charmers have trapped me as well. And, I must confess, I am a hopeless and willing victim.

The anticipation of capture and the hunger to possess, overwhelms me. I cannot ignore the tattered orphans that beckon me from their roadside lairs. Silently, relentlessly, tauntingly, they burrow into my psyche and demand my attention.

From their pavement perches they appear forlorn; awaiting their fates. But, it is a trick. They are perfect in their shabbiness and impossible to resist.

I hesitate. Make a snap decision—as I knew I would—and then I stop ... every time.

Stiletto Heels

My attire is never appropriate for this type of roadside spontaneity. But then, I'm weak, and the adrenaline rush of capturing another prize over-rides my Diva pride.

My bumper sticker reads ... 'Caution! Diva on Board!'

Reeling with anticipation, I scramble out of my vehicle, intent on stalking my prey; ready to add another rescued relic to my collection.

Then, from the recesses of my mind, the Diva starts transmitting her cautionary alarms. Annoyed, I brush her aside. I am being reminded that I might ruin my evening shoes in the snow and slush that entomb my prize. Irritated, I shut her down, fully aware that sensibility will never override my delight in the hunt or dim the steely-eyed focus of this huntress.

After my prey is snatched from its frozen, roadside grave, I give it a cursory inspection, smile naughtily, and heave it into my car.

It fits.

I offer a quick prayer, thankful that I didn't have to hoist my prize onto my car carrier and turn to continue my journey.

Climbing back into my vehicle, I fumble in the dark for my car kit, find my hand wipes and spend a quick moment removing the grunge from my hands and shoes. Slathering my lips with another layer of gloss, I headed toward my event ... damned pleased with how the evening is progressing.

When shopping for thrift, be prepared to embrace the unknown and value the unexpected.

Chapter 6

The Art of "RE"

P eople who willingly stand knee-deep in the vast ocean of thrift must also surrender to a life of *RE*. Most thrift hunters enjoy the process of RE-storing, RE-newing, RE-purposing, RE-using, RE-vamping, RE-finishing, RE-fining, and RE-designing.

Watch out!
A Diva wielding
a hammer is not
a good thing . . .
even if it is pink.

The prefix "RE" simply means again or back; using something again or bringing an item back to life.

Many of the pieces that I have found on my thrifting adventures have been worn, marred or broken, which is why I have been able to get them so cheap. The hidden possibilities within these damaged beings always inspire me, igniting my creative fires.

Somehow stuff just seems to find me; similar to a mongrel that wanders onto a property and claims the land—and the house—as its own. I've refurbished items friends have given me, treasures I have found along the roadside, and damaged or marred objects picked up at local flea markets and thrift shops.

Refurbishing thrift is more than an art form ... is is a belief;
a creative endeavor which involves not only the **hunt,**
but the certainty that under the grunge of every tattered
find, a treasure is waiting to be born.

Novice thrifters typically pass over the very items that I snap up at bargain prices. I, however, have learned to turn them into unique, functional pieces which eventually find a place in my home or, in some cases, my next garage sale.

The renovation and restoration processes are (almost) as enjoyable as the hunt. I've found that fixing broken parts, applying a fresh coat of paint or simply rubbing an item down with a good, lifesaving oil is a therapeutic endeavor.

I'm also a collector of parts: crystal bottle stoppers, unique stands, boxes, distinctive tops and ceramic bowls.

Occasionally, I raid my store of goods and construct an imaginative display.

In this example, I placed a midsized piece of pottery atop tri-footed brass holder, then selected a unique top to fit the hand-thrown basin. This is one of my favortite creations, made from a bunch of orphaned parts. Total cost … $6.00!

The First Aid Kit

To organize my supplies, and make the restoration process easier, I purchased an 18" x 18" x 30" portable supply cart-on-wheels to hold my necessary repair items. This mobile kit can easily be hoisted into my car or moved around my house as needed.

From time to time, I find that it's easier to work on my projects late at night after the household is fast asleep. During these stolen hours I push my kit and the wounded waifs in front of the television and begin the restoration process.

The ritual of breathing new life into derelict castoffs is therapeutic. I love to give birth—or rebirth—to things that have been carelessly tossed away; rendered useless ... forgotten soldiers. The rejuvenation process feeds me, nourishing my soul.

I believe that thrift is essential to well-ordered living.
~ **John D. Rockefeller**

Insider Secrets

Over the years products have come and gone. Some make their way into my repair kit only to lose favor and end up being replaced by a newer or better version.

Today, I rely on 20 effective products:

- *Old English Scratch Remover* – I'm so in love with this product. Next to my black permanent marker, this item is the most used utensil in my kit. Stripping furniture is way too much work.

  This miracle worker hides scratches and mars superbly. And, it brings out the beauty of a piece without losing the charm of its wear and tear.

- **Cheesecloth** – Saturated, oil laden cloths were the bane of my vampy little existence until I discovered ... cheesecloth. This material allows most of the oil to saturate the wood rather than the cloth. Hallelujah!

- **Permanent Markers** – A set of colorful, vibrant pens has claimed its place as my favorite touchup buddy. These lively sticks are magical; neatly hiding a glut of flaws and nicks on ceramic, leather, wood and cloth. However, the most sued marker in my kit is black, followed closely by the metallics; gold, silver, and bronze.

  Permanent markers are a mainstay of my refurbishing hobby and I invest in several sets. This is one of the few times I will pay retail as I have never found them at garage sales. (Heaven help me!)
- **String and Rubber Bands** – Use these handy binders to secure a variety of loose items.
- **Clamps** – These nifty holders are essential for holding several components together while glue or paint is drying. Clamps come in small, medium and large sizes.
- **Tape** – Tape is a great quick fix. Keep a roll of scotch, masking, electrical, and duct tape handy to use on a variety of projects.
- **Stapler** – A heavy duty stapler is my mainstay when changing fabric on furniture. Refitting a chair with a lively piece of material is the extent of my knowledge and maximum commitment to the reupholstering process. I pass on items that require a professional.

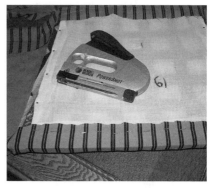

- **Glue** – Adhesives have been manufactured to specifically bond wood, glass, plastic or metal. After years of trying every creation made, I finally decided to stick with three bonding agents exclusively:

White glue – This bonding agent is a fantastic multi-purpose fixative that holds well and is almost invisible when dry.

Wood glue – *Titebond Wood Glue* has been around for years, is reliable, and a superb adhesive for attaching wood to wood. It sets quickly, and if the excess is wiped up, leaves little telltale residue when dry.

Specialty glue – *Elmer's Ultimate High Performance Glue* has the best adhesion for holding together different materials. This product is a little tricky because it is applied with water and expands as it sets. The excess glue that seeps out between the cracks needs to be wiped off as it dries, but the adhesion is superior, and the area can be sanded and painted.

A lovely oriental brass holder with a carved bone handle was in two pieces when I purchased it at a thrift shop for a couple of bucks. The handle was completely separated from the deeply tarnished brass base, obviously corroded from years of neglect.

After cleaning the brass, I applied a mixture of *Elmer's Ultimate Glue* and water. The mixture immediately began to expand and adhere. Over the next 15 minutes I painstakingly wiped the oozing adhesive glue away from the connecting seam until the expansion ceased.

The holder was set aside to season for 24 hours and the *object de art* revealed no trace of repair.

- **Glue Remover** – Removing price tags and their residue is the bane of my Diva existence. Thrift stores have a knack for peppering their merchandise with a surplus of tags. So. I must perform the ardous task of removing them ... begrudgingly. However, I did find a great little product called *Oops* that wipes those sticky buggers off instantly.

- **Artist Brushes** – Fine-bristled brushes are used to re-paint areas that my permanent markers are just too coarse to handle, such as marks on paintings, frames, boxes, and ceramics.
- **Oil Paints and Watercolors** – A set of small paints used to fill in chips will last for years as long as I squeeze the paint to the end and tighten the caps.
- **Batteries** – I despise having to get up to rummage around for a battery when I'm working on a project, so I keep a supply handy. A timely tip that prevents returning items that don't work is to carry four AA and two AAA batteries when shopping. Slip them into items to see if they work right on the spot. This trick eliminates a lot of returns and disappointment.
- **Light Bulbs** – I keep one 100-watt bulb and one 60-watt bulb in my kit, along with one small-necked bulb to test repaired lights. Timesaving tip: I carry the smallest light bulb I can find during thrifting jaunts to test out lamps.
- **Cotton Swabs** – These helpers are great for cleaning, oiling or coloring the small cracks and crevices in furniture and decor. Sometimes years of grime need to be cleaned away and these handy dabbers get the job done.
- **Felt Squares** – Since I move décor around … a lot, I line the bottoms of my accessories with felt squares to protect the furniture and floors.
- **Velcro Tape** – This ingenious product was developed in the late 40s (Yes, it's been around that long). I use these super-grippers to attach a variety of items, one to another.
- **Needle and Thread** – Sewing, or more specifically repair work, is a thankless but necessary part of the restoration process. There is little satisfaction in mending; simply because an effective repair is almost invisible.

- **Paint Sticks** – These handy touch-up paints, in pen form, are useful for dabbing bits of color onto chipped frames, ceramics, and décor pieces.
- **Magnifying Glass** – As I grow gracefully older, magnifying glasses are used to examine, paint, or repair tiny items. I even boast a large table magnifier as well as a small handheld piece.

Paleeze . . . If I ever have to use a magnifying glass, I hope whatever I'm trying to see is worth the embarrassment.

- **Cleaning Products** – Glass cleaner, all-purpose wipes, paper towels and clean rags are always stored in the sides of my kit for easy access.

My heart starts to palpitate when I see an open sign at a thrift store. Especially, an uncharted one I've never seen before.
~ **Elizabeth Mason**

Chapter 7

Bargains
and Baubles

T he All-American garage sale has become a spring and summer tradition, peppering the entrepreneurial alleyways of this country with the heady excitement of resale.

These events, commonly referred to as garage sales, yard sales, tags sales, or moving sales, offer a wide range of secondhand goods in various states and conditions.

In the warmer climes, where merchandise is sold from yards and driveways, the events are referred to as *Yard Sales.* In the east they are called *Tag Sales.* And, in the northern regions, where shelter is often needed, sellers display their wares inside their garages, thus earning the term *Garage Sale.*

Most of these homespun events are held on weekends, where household items are displayed after a home has been purged and all the castoffs have been rounded up and tagged.

Sellers attempt to attract as many people as possible in hopes of ridding homes of unneccessary, or unwanted goods.

Items put on the auction block, so to speak, range from new, to like-new, to usable. Typically, the seller no longer needs or wants the items, is attempting to de-clutter, needs to downsize, or is simply trying to raise funds.

The thrift business is booming! From first-time apartment decorators to feisty baby boomers choosing to change their lairs, the thrift craze has all sorts of folks scouring secondhand venues for cheap alternatives to mainstream retail.

Used products are sold from porches, lawns, driveways, garages, carports, and on occasion, from inside a home. Some sellers, unkindly referred to as *squatters*, take their wares to busy locations to sell from their vehicles. The most common reason for this transient practice is their subdivisions do not allow sales or their homes are located in remote areas.

Advertising attempts for these weekend sales run the gamut from simple signs posted at the corners of the seller's subdivision to a full-blown campaign composed of signs, flyers, Internet posts, and newspaper ads.

Despite the methods used to sell secondhand goods, this great American pastime is appealing to a growing number of enthusiasts. From those endorsing the greening of America to harried housewives looking to make some additional pin money, the craze is gaining momentum.

Yikes! Did I really say "pin money?" Well, that term just aged me about 30 years.

Garage Sales

Garage sales are wonderful bargain troves and, when in season, I typically prefer to shop these homespun sales versus thrift stores or flea markets.

My reasoning is fairly sound; they tend to be run by newbies who are more interested in getting rid of their castoffs than in making huge profits.

I have found some of my best deals from the junk-strewn sales of these enterprising peddlers.

The Ritzy Side of Town

Identifying and locating vintage items or unique pieces can be a challenge. I scout out certain sections of town to locate the specific things I am seeking. For example, older neighborhoods are great for finding vintage fashions and fifties décor or memorabilia. Many of the residents are retired or moving, and their sales offer a surplus of old costume jewelry, kitchenware and furniture, great clothing and collectables.

On the other hand, the ritzy neighborhoods abound with designer clothing, art and décor, new and almost new household items, great furniture and leftovers from remodeling projects.

To find the best selections, I hit the sales early, bargain like crazy (because it is expected), and always bring cash since most sellers do not accept checks.

The hunt is addictive. It's easy to get hooked on this elusive quest. One day I might fill my car with a host of potential treasures while the next day is a complete bust. But then ... there's always the next weekend!

Diva Don'ts

There are challenges associated with locating and buying from these homespun sales. In my search for the perfect find, some "greenhorn" practices drive me batty:

1. **Advertising efforts that are ineffective or amateurish, making finding sales difficult**

2. **Sales held for a single day**

3. **Curtailed hours (i.e. 10:00 a.m. to 2:00 p.m.)**

4. **Dirty, disorganized merchandise**

I include *moving sales* in the garage sale category, and kiddingly refer to them as *motivated garage sales*. These desperate events have all the attributes of a normal garage sale, except for the fact that the people are moving. They are typically very keen on selling their stuff ... quickly. Understandably, they are reluctant to pay a moving company to transport things that they no longer want or need. These sellers are ready to bargain!

Be vigilant.
Seize the moment.
March into the fray!
Hmm, where's my
hairspray?

Demolition Sales

Whenever I am in the remodeling or building mode, I scout out the demolition sales in my area. Incredible deals can be had for a song when owners demolish their properties in order to build a newer or larger structure.

Before the site is razed, everything is put up for sale: from flooring to windows and doors to the proverbial kitchen sink. Brass fixtures, ornate fireplace mantles and stunning light fixtures are all sold for pennies on the dollar. Quality wood casings, moldings and flooring that would otherwise be unaffordable, sell at rock bottom prices.

Demolition sales are typically well attended and buyers are extremely focused and intense; they know exactly what they are looking for and make their decisions quickly.

Whenever I attend these sales, I work fast, make my choices and pay for the items I wish to purchase. After all transactions are completed, the buyers usually have several days to remove their merchandise.

Subdivision Sales

Multi-home subdivision sales are a sheer delight. When shopping from these busy bargain streets, I'm as happy as a kid in a candy store. I'm saving time and maximizing my buying opportunities. For ardent thrifters, these extravaganzas can easily eat up a full day of trotting from house to house.

Participating homes often carry subdivision maps indicating which homes in the neighborhood are open for business.

My fave . . . subdivision sales! They are the ultimate, never-ending garage sale, giving new meaning to the phrase "Shop till you drop."

Held in the spring and fall, these extravaganzas often involve as many as 30 to 60 homes selling everything from used furniture to automobiles and campers. Furniture, décor, appliances, art, tools, as well as garden, patio and office equipment are displayed in varying states; strewn across lawns, piled on card tables or stacked on makeshift shelving. Although prices are generally cheap, I still bargain. Sellers are aware of the heavy competition, and realize that the house right next door might be making better deals! If I don't like the prices at one house, the one right next door might just make me a better deal.

Estate Sales

Estate sales or estate liquidation sales are events designed to dispose of the personal property of an individual who is recently deceased. In some cases the sellers must divest themselves of their possessions in order to move.

These organized sales run the gamut from family members selling furnishings and household items to a team of professional liquidators offering up the contents of a palatial estate.

Regardless of the venue, estate sales usually have goods that are higher quality than thrift shops or garage sales. Therefore, I typically attend these secondhand bonanzas on the last day of the sale when the sellers are more willing to bargain. Some companies will drastically slash prices the last hours of a sale. Now we're talking!

I get my Bling fix whenever I attend estate sales. They are right up my little Diva alley.

Below is an example of an ad that promoted daily and even hourly discounts:

> ## Terms and Conditions of the Estate Sale:
> **Wednesday: 2:30pm – 6pm**
> **Thursday – Friday, 9am – 4pm**
> **Saturday Clearance: 9am – 2pm — 50% OFF**
> **2:01pm – 5pm — 75% OFF**

The best merchandise is typically snatched up on the first day, but later I can still find great bargains by working a little harder and looking at things with an imaginative eye. When I do find something with potential, I have trained myself to focus on the possibilities of the object rather than the flaws.

Recently, I purchased a handsome carved wood mirror for $50 at an estate sale just minutes before closing. After taking a quick tour of the

house, I spotted a large mirror leaning against a wall in the living room. It still had the original receipt attached to it, so I knew that the retail price was $419 and that the estate was asking $125 for it.

I had also noted, from a sign posted at the front door, that everything was 50 percent off, bringing the cost of the mirror down to $62.50. With that in mind, I made an offer of $50. It was accepted. Feeling victorious, I proudly packed that beauty up ... and took her home.

I love the quality of the merchandise at estate sales. But, even these treasure troves have their limitations.

- Their sale days are limited—opening their doors for just two or three days.
- Their quality and prices are typically higher than the thrifty finds uncovered at either garage sales or thrift shops.
- These events, often professionally run, are usually crowded and patronized by savvy buyers.

Therefore, I'm decisive and will buy only if the price is right. In the end, I work with the knowledge that the good stuff will go first, my choices are limited and there are no duplicates hanging out in the back room.

The Living Estate Sale

Today, I advertise my sales as *Living Estate Sales* versus *Garage Sales*. There are several reasons for this shift:

1. My merchandise progressively improved each ensuing year as I diligently purged my home of things I did not need or absolutely love.

2. A great deal of time was spent staging my sale, realizing people love to shop in nice settings.

My merchandise is so fab, I'm tempted to buy it from myself.

3. Since I've only moved four times in the past 30 years, I hesitate to call my events *Moving Sales*.

4. And, I sure didn't want to call them *Estate Sales*, since the last I checked … I hadn't died.

So, I was in a quandary. What should I call my special events?

It was during one of my figuring-it-all-out periods that I read a clever ad written by two women who had a ton of really cool things to sell. They explained that no one had died and that they were simply ridding their homes of a truckload of designer furniture: décor, art, household items and clothing. I was excited to go to their sale because the ad was so ingenious and alluring.

The weekend was jam-packed. And, these gals had the knack for creating a fun, party-like atmosphere. Their sale items were exceptional and prices were moderate to high. Both scurried from customer to customer like little helper bees.

They were mistresses of social interaction: talking, laughing and kibitzing. It was obvious that the shoppers were having a good time and that these women knew how to mix mingling with selling.

I was hooked. Since that sale, I have called my events *Living Estate Sales.*

The following ad is one I ran on Craigslist for a recent sale. Notice that I tell people that the merchandise is high-end. I don't want dollar shoppers to expect to buy beautiful, quality items for pennies. The copy is very similar to that of an Estate Sale except for one significant fact...no one died.

You can bet your sweet little booties baby . . . this Diva is alive and kicking!

A FABULOUS "LIVING" ESTATE SALE!

Rain or Shine
THURSDAY- SATURDAY
9:00-5:00

DECORATOR IS CLEANING HOUSE!

EVERYTHING MUST GO!

IF YOU ARE DECORATING, RE-DECORATING
OR JUST LOVE TO SHOP... THIS IS THE PLACE
FOR FABULOUS FINDS!
UNLIKE ANY SALE YOU'VE EVER SEEN!
BEAUTIFUL, QUALITY ITEMS

- Fabulous VINTAGE BED – Full
- FURNITURE and ANTIQUES
- PATIO SET – TABLE, 5 CHAIRS, 2 ROCKERS, UMBRELLA
- MIRRORS
- LAMPS, LAMPS, & LAMPS
- Gorgeous ART
- Elegant DÉCOR
- Fresh LINENS
- CONFERENCE TABLE
- KITCHEN ITEMS (for the gourmet cook)

JOIN IN THE FUN AT: ADDRESS - DATE - TIMES

Antique Shops and Malls

Like most thrift venues, antique shops run the gamut from high-end, well-appointed stores to filled-to-the-brim establishments pushing everything from Betty Boop paraphernalia to bowling balls.

These intriguing concerns are favored by vintage aficionados and collectors of mementos from bygone eras.

Most establishments are run by educated sellers that know the value of their merchandise ... and the prices markets will bear. Although a shopper can usually find the very things they've been searching for, the prices will most likely be reflective of an item's book value.

On a recent cross-country trip, I came across a fun shop nestled on a corner of historic Route 66 in Amarillo, Texas.

In that bustling town, Clint Culwell, an entertaining proprietor, runs an eclectic enterprise called Seven Brothers Mercantile (*www.SevenBros.com*). I spent several contented hours browsing his busy establishment that literally bulged with novelties and memorabilia.

His online store, boasting *Modern Merchandise with Old-Fashioned Value*, sells everything from American flags to pirates' plunder.

Thrift Stores

I'm a big fan of thrift stores because products change daily, stores are open year 'round, they commonly operate seven days a week, their prices are low to moderate and much of their proceeds go to charity.

When shopping at these establishments, my goal is to schedule my arrival as soon as the doors open so as to catch the new merchandise that was put out the night before or early in the morning.

Whether national chains or mom and pop businesses, these outlets are great resources for clothing and common household items such as cookware, glasses, linens, blankets, home décor and small appliances.

I also patronize the *half-off days* that thrift stores are famous for. As a matter-of-fact, I have been thrifting for so long that I now buy only when a thrift store is running a special to assure that I'm getting the best deals.

Shopping for furniture at these concerns can be dicey since most people sell their better pieces through consignment shops, estate sales, auctions, or Craigslist.

However, thrift stores will, on occasion, display goods from a donor who wants to divest themselves of all assets. It is obvious that these folks have neither the time nor the inclination to run a sale.

Running across these surprising bonanzas is what makes thrift store shopping so much fun.

The thrift business is booming! From first-time apartment dwellers to the downsizing baby boomers, the thrift craze has all sorts of folks scouring the secondhand venues for fabulous finds.

Yes, many of my visits go unrewarded, and I have to sift through a lot of junk to find the exceptional pieces. However, I don't have to find something every time I shop to get excited about the possibilities that lurk beneath the heaps of discarded rubble.

The thrift store chains in my town are open for business every day. Mmmm, that's music to my Bling bedecked ears!

Thrift stores are fun and arguably a treasure hunter's feast, which keeps this thrifty Diva coming back for more.

Today, leading a more frugal existence has turned into big business for the national thrift store chains. With a downturn in the economy, people are catching on to the huge advantages of living a thrifty and green lifestyle.

Consignment Shops

The consignment model affords an opportunity for people to buy gently used furniture and household items at greatly reduced prices.

These resale environments range from pleasant to opulent and offer an array of beautifully displayed merchandise.

Purveyors of secondhand goods price their wares markedly below new and often mix gently used items with brand new merchandise.

The selling arrangement holds the consignee (seller) responsible for displaying and selling the merchandise for the consignor (person who owns the item). Typically, a portion of each sale is paid to the consignor.

A very talented friend of mine opened a consignment shop called *Fun Finds and Designs.* This trendy establishment is nestled in the small, bedroom community of Canton, Georgia. The shop has flourished under the artful guidance of its owner, Betty Anderson, decorator extraordinaire. Visiting her website, *www.FunFindsAndDesigns.com,* the viewer is privy to decorating tips, what sells and what just sits.

Consignment shops differ from charity or thrift shops in that people commission the store caretakers to sell their goods, and each party receives a percentage of the sales.

I've spent many hours wandering the halls of these beautifully merchandised establishments and have found that most often the items are of high quality. When I buy, I'm always mindful that the prices are higher because commissions are shared.

Flea Markets

Flea markets are held outdoors, in parks or within the roped off sections of parking lots. These festive events are usually held on weekends throughout the year (or during the summer months in the northern regions).

Vendors set up their wares under a tent or awning, sheltering products that range from antique to gently-used to brand new. The atmosphere is jovial, haggling is the norm, the goods are plentiful, and great treasures await the imaginative shopper.

Auctions

Anything that one can imagine or might ever want or need is sold at auction. Cars, office equipment, jewelry, houses and entire estates are just a few of the items that make the bid lists of these fast paced events.

An auction is simply a group of buyers and collectors that bid against each other to obtain an object that ultimately goes to the highest bidder.

Auctions are one of the fastest ways to move used furniture, antiques and décor. However, if you are the seller, the price of your merchandise is dependent upon what a buyer is willing to pay at any given moment. Unlike estate sales, garage sales, or even consignment shops, auctions typically ensure that all items will be sold.

I never go to auctions anymore; they scare the bejeebers out of me. One afternoon I adjusted my hat and ended up with a 1950's Rolls Royce!

There are auctions that let the seller place a minimum bid on their own merchandise, while other houses allow the vendor to buy their items back at the house's percentage.

Many people are intimidated by auctions because they don't know what to expect. It may take attending a few of these events to drop any hesitation and enjoy the lively banter and rapid bidding process.

To ease the apprehension surrounding these fast-paced events, I do a search on the Internet for auctions that carry the type of merchandise I'm looking for; usually one that offers a relaxed environment.

A great resource for finding local, live auctions is *www.AuctionZip.com.* When I first started to attend these lively bidding wars, I was a spectator … getting comfortable with the process. It was only after I felt safe that I began to bid.

There are many types of auctions to choose from:

- Online auctions list bidders by a screen name, and offer a wide variety of enticing goods. Patience is required as it can take time for items of interest to come up for bid.

  Because these events are online, they do not allow bidders to handle or examine the merchandise, which can increase the chances of buying poor or damaged goods.

  Posted merchandise is usually on the bidding list for a week. The process always starts off slow and bidding speeds up as the deadline draws near.

- High-end auction houses like Sotheby's and Christie's are typically attended by seasoned, wealthy bidders. Their catalogs are diverse, usually high-end, and typically display antiques and collectable items.

- Country auctions are informal functions that move varied items ranging from furniture to farm equipment. These lively events progress quickly and their inventory historically sells for a fraction of its original cost.

Auctions can last from a few hours to several days. When entire estates are auctioned off, bidders are allowed to preview the stock or collections before the auction starts. This system allows shoppers the opportunity to inspect the merchandise and decide on their personal bid limits. It also prevents a bidder from getting swept up in the competitiveness and excitement of the moment.

Most live auctions require registration where a fee is collected in exchange for a bidding number. During the auction, the bidding goes quite fast, so it is wise to make sure that the auctioneers or their assistants are aware of you when offering bids. When in doubt, I stand up until I get the nod that they have taken my bid.

In the end, I simply have fun enjoying the entertainment, the camaraderie, and the fast pace of this great pastime.

Thrift on the Internet

With the downward spiral of the economy, families are more prudent with their spending practices. People who would never have considered secondhand resources are turning toward the various thrift outlets to furnish their homes and clothe their families.

Tag sales, estate sales, thrift stores, antique malls and consignment shops are all reporting huge increases in traffic. At the same time, bargain hunters are turning to the Internet in droves. Whether scrolling through Craigslist, *www.Craigslist.com*, poring over the plentiful garage sale listings at *www.gsalr.com* or scouring the many locations for local thrift shops, *www.ThriftShopper.com*, frugal shoppers are realizing the feast offered by these user-friendly online resources.

New resources are popping up weekly because thrifting has turned into an accepted pursuit, while secondhand trappings are becoming quite chic.

Chapter 8

Thrift Etiquette

What? Have we all gone mad? A code of behavior for *thrifters*? Well, yes. It actually makes sense. In the retail world there is seldom a fight for merchandise ... unlike the rivalry for one-of-a-kind finds at the various thrift venues. From garage sales to auctions, competition for quality items can be fierce.

When I first started to shop the thrift venues, I never thought there were unwritten, but strictly observed, thrifting laws.

Newbie shoppers, in their haste to check out the goods, tend to forget simple manners. Veteran thrifters, in large part, are aware of the unwritten protocol that surrounds these intense buying binges. Therefore, the novice bargain hunter would be wise to learn and adhere to the unwritten protocol before venturing into this frugal terrain.

A few timely tips to get started on the right foot:

- Pick up or examine any item that is worth consideration. While the piece is in your possession, make the decision to buy or not. Once an object is abandoned, it is fair game for the next shopper.
- Practice patience. If someone is examining an item you think you want ... walk away. Hovering can trigger impulse buying.

Grrr, go ahead, try to take my bone!

Thrifters are very territorial and standing next to them, or even admiring the object in question, can activate the purchase of an item that they might otherwise pass on.

After losing great finds to my competition, I learned not to show any interest in items that others were considering.

Today I casually walk away, wait my turn from a distance and busy myself while keeping an eye on the other shopper. If the competing shopper sets the item down, I rush over, pick it up and reclaim my prize.

After observing dog behavior over the years, I dare say ... possession is, irretrievably, nine-tenths of the law.

- Be friendly and helpful. Share information and chat about other sales, specials, directions, or area information.
- Courtesy goes a long way. Good sales are busy sales so it is prudent to respect the natural flow of things; long checkout lines, piles of hold items stacked for future sales, areas that are off limits, and stressed workers that are hard pressed to be helpful.
- Park respectfully. This may mean down the street or even around the corner. Don't obstruct people from entering or leaving. And, avoid parking in driveways as these areas are reserved for the handicapped or loading and unloading.
- Be neat and respectful of property that still belongs to the seller. Having held many sales, I know how much work it takes to keep things tidy. Therefore, I appreciate customers who refold, re-hang and replace items they are considering, or might eventually decide against.

A Thrift Diva is always courteous but plays "Let's Make A Deal" ... like a pro!

Chapter 9

Haggling
with the Haggler

Dickering over price is expected ... especially on the last day of a sale. While new buyers may land some great deals, it is important that they also remain in the good graces of the seller.

- Be true to your word. When making an offer, follow through and purchase the item if the amount offered is accepted by the seller.

- Get comfortable with the counter offer. In addition, it is appropriate to counter again if the seller comes back with a price that you feel is too high.

I'll never forget one starlit night when a handsome stranger told me that I need to know when to walk away.

Now, what do you think that cute, little Kenny Rogers meant by that?

- Know when to walk away. If a counter offer isn't accepted by the seller, the buyer has the right to politely refuse to buy the object.
- Haggle with integrity. If a counter offer is accepted, the buyer should be committed to purchasing the item.
- Buy in bulk. Sellers will often discount an entire purchase if a buyer is willing to take multiple pieces. Therefore, gather all potential items together to make a deal.

- Make offers with cash in hand. Some veteran bargain hunters contend that most people respond favorably to a visual display of money held out to them when making an offer. These experts contend that people are hard pressed to refuse the lure of ready cash.

- Respect a seller's pricing. When making an offer, I usually ask, "What's the best that you will do on this item?" or "Will you take this amount for these pieces?"
- Get creative. If a seller isn't willing to bargain on a piece, I quickly calculate what other things might be used to seal the deal. For example, I have often suggested that I would buy an article if the seller would be so kind as to help me load the item into my

vehicle, deliver goods to my home, or clean up a piece before loading it into my car. People are very willing to offer their services if it means getting rid of things they no longer need or want. In the end, they get their price and I take home a great find that was loaded or cleaned. Nice. A win-win transaction.

Once a born-again thrifter has acclimated to shopping at discount stores and thrift venues, she is less likely to revert back to her earlier behaviors: impulse buying, paying full retail price and excessive consumerism.

Chapter 10

The Great Junk Roundup

I was a junk-aholic. The excuses, rationalizations, symptoms and signs were all there. But the last one to see them was me.

It was tough taking responsibility for my collecting, but at some level I knew I needed to become responsible and take charge of my life—or rather take it back.

Clutter builds stress. I knew that. But I opted to live with overflowing drawers, closets that avalanched clothes and cluttered rooms. Partnering with those silent tension builders, I grew immune to their destructive forces ... or thought I had.

Getting Tough

I really am an organizational junkie. But because of my ardent collecting, guests that surveyed my home during those thrift-a-maniac years would have thought otherwise.

The art of collecting, I had mastered. What I hadn't learned how to do was flush out all the unwanted and unnecessary stuff that magically and constantly appeared; junk that pressed against my space and cluttered my mind.

Granted, I had accumulated beautiful things, but, if the truth be told, I was attached to my stuff. I had yet to realize the exquisite freedom inherent in release ... the unfettered bliss of letting go.

I struggled to find balance, hoping to rid myself of the chaos that churned through my life. It was obvious that I had chosen to spend my time hunting and restoring rather than clearing and sorting.

Too much clutter puts me over the edge, but I've found that chocolate helps.

My years of thrifting and failure to keep up with the growing mountain of sorting, storing and purging, eventually brought me to my knees.

Oh, I had my "story" down pat, all right. I used every pathetic excuse I could drum up to justify my inaction; *I don't know what to do with all my stuff. Work is just too demanding right now. You don't understand; another project just might put me over the edge.*

To make matters worse, my mischievous sprites were working overtime. Quietly, consistently, relentlessly, they toyed with my head, urging me to change my frazzled life. I knew, at many levels, that I was drained by all the chaos; fed up with the inner turmoil. I needed a reprieve.

Although my private battles continued to rage, inch by inch my warrior spirit pulled me closer to sanity, allowing the rising tide of order and good sense to surface.

After all, I'm a Virgo. Stamped indelibly on my forehead is a complete set of instructions accompanied by a feisty pair of internal gremlins; a set of psychological clutter-busters that were hell bent on getting me organized. A platoon of orderly soldiers. Liberators of havoc. Tension relievers.

It was only after I got good and mad . . . that clarity arrived.

Looking around at my disarray and sick to the core of my disheveled life, I took on the manner of Howard Beal in the movie *Network* (1976). Standing on my tippy toes, I shouted, *I'm mad as hell and I'm not going to take it anymore!*

Thar's Gold in Them Thar Cupboards

After I pulled my feet out of the deep mire of self-talk and recrimination, I committed to a thorough purge of my house.

Steadfast in my resolve, I swore that I would toss every unnecessary, unused or unloved article from my home. Weary of the chaos, I longed for all that the home and garden magazines promised; a harmonious dwelling brimming with order and tranquility.

The picture of my own tidy sanctuary began to materialize despite all the chaos in my brain. I lay in bed imagining the transformation; the great purge, a lively garage sale, buying fabulous pieces of thrift and the great makeover of my home.

The precarious side to my wistful dreaming was my wobbly financial state. Finding some extra cash was no small matter.

While divesting myself of all the unwanted things that had been suffocating me, I began to understand that there were unrealized riches hidden in my cupboards and closets. My house was bursting with money waiting to be claimed, and it was the thought of that ready cash that propelled me forward.

The Great Divide

Although new to the game, I realized that the first purge was going to take time. I bowed to the fact, realizing that what took years to build would take months to divest.

With that thought in mind, I set aside three months to de-clutter my home in preparation for my first garage sale.

My house was divided into little, easy to swallow bites—workable parameters. On paper, I partitioned it into sections, breaking it down by room:

- Kitchen
- Living room
- Dining room
- Bedrooms
- Bathrooms
- Laundry room
- Family room or porch
- Basement
- Garage

From there, each room was divided further into smaller, reasonable sections:

- Cupboards
- Shelves
- Hutches and armoires
- Closets
- Drawers
- Bookcases
- Storage areas

The process of breaking things into small portions served me well. I could imagine tackling a drawer, or a cupboard. It made sense. It was feasible. And, in the end, these smaller tasks saved me from backing away from my resolve.

The Good, the Bad and the Ugly

Once I got started with clearing my clutter, indecision haunted me. Overwhelmed with uncertainty I stewed over each piece. Should I keep it? Would I need it? Would I miss it?

There were too many choices to make during that painful clearing process. I hadn't anticipated that I would be paralyzed with indecision.

Realizing that I was at a turning point, I decided to create a set of criteria that would allow me to make instant decisions and not waste time stewing over each "coveted" piece.

If undecided about an item, I simply keep in mind what that old fogy Aristotle said ... Nature abhors a vacuum!

So, Diva-logic interprets that to mean, whenever I get rid of something ... I get to SHOP!

In determining what to keep and what to toss, I put each piece to a test:

- Had I used the item in the last year?
- Would I buy it again if I were to donate or throw it away?
- Does the piece have sentimental value, as in a family treasure?

By putting each questionable item through this assessment, I found it easier to stay on track. And, as one might imagine, the article in question, usually lost the bet.

Brass Tacks

Every closet and drawer was tackled, one pull at a time. Working in small increments and de-cluttering each workable area, I felt relief wash over me. It felt good. Order and stability were returning along with a heady sense of accomplishment.

As I worked, I placed all of the items I wasn't keeping into one of three boxes: *Sell, Donate,* or *Trash.* Everything that I wanted to keep was put—neatly—back into its original space.

My goal of course was to sell most of the hidden junk, the things that had gone unnoticed for years.

Cleaning and Tagging

By committing to one small, achievable project every day; purging a drawer, a closet, an armoire, a hutch or even a section of a room, the house gradually became structured and organized.

However, a huge collection of boxes, overflowing with a mishmash of sale articles, was starting to pile up. I realized that I would soon be confronted with the herculean task of cleaning, pricing and sorting if I didn't start processing each box as I went along.

I changed direction in mid-stream. Once a carton of discards had been collected, I hauled it in front of a TV

Now that we're on the topic of cleaning, I contend that nothing good has ever come from the sound of rubber gloves being snapped firmly into place.

where I cleaned, tagged, and priced each item. This effort served two purposes; it gave me a break from all the pricing decisions (which were taking their toll), and each piece was readied for the sale.

This system proved to be as beneficial in saving time as it was com-

forting to my bruised psyche. At least I knew I wouldn't be faced with an enormous pricing job the day before the sale.

Once packed, each box was marked according to its contents and stored in the basement, porch or under a tarp in the back yard.

Knowing that my next area to purge would be the garage, I did not want to add more boxes to that chaotic beast. Clearing it would be challenging enough without adding more junk to its contents.

Therefore, marked boxes were stored in other areas waiting the eventual cleaning and sorting that would precede the creation of my *Garage Boutique*.

Yikes ...

The time had come to tackle the biggest mess in my home. With great trepidation I yanked open the garage door. My resolve waivered as I stared at the stacks of unwanted jumble heaped in topsy-turvy disarray throughout the dreary interior.

A storm of uncertainty hit me. The only thing that saved me from slamming the door and scurrying back into my organized home was the month I had spent agonizing over each piece I had tossed.

There was no turning back.

I had done too much work to give up now. Despite my hesitation, I knew, in order to tame this monster, I would have to break it into workable parts.

Eventually, every item, every scrap of wood, rusted tool and orphaned screw was considered, donated, tossed or readied for the sale.

In the end, my plan worked. By leaving the biggest task for last and breaking it into small increments, I got the job done.

Standing back after months of work, I celebrated the completion of my massive project. Pleased, I blissfully let the restoring sense of accomplishment wash over me.

Life is simply a series of decisions; the better the decision, the more fluid the life.

Div-a-Chi

The flow of positive energy or *Chi* that coursed through my freshly purged home was delicious. I basked in its therapeutic force and embraced its tangible energy.

I was beginning to realize that there were more benefits to this de-cluttering thing than I had imagined.

- I had a clean, organized home … and that felt great.
- My environmental stress was gone … vanished.
- My efforts were rewarded by a sense of accomplishment.
- I gained time. Everything in my home now had a place, allowing me to find things, quickly.
- My castoffs would soon be sold to yield immediate cash in hand.
- And, it tickled me to think that someone would love my old, discarded stuff … and pay to have it.

The Mule Stance

I work with people all the time that yearn for a lovely, harmonious home, despite the fact that they choose to live in clutter haven. Just the thought of purging their dwellings lowers them into an abyss of paralytic indecision.

I've witnessed strong competent women turned into whiney, sniveling protesters when faced with the prospect of de-cluttering their homes or organizing a tag sale.

I just think of purging as a little bump in the road on my shopping journey.

If in the final analysis indecision continues to be perplexing, think in terms of what is more important ... the item or the cash in hand.

Some folks are so overwhelmed by the sheer size of the task, they simply dig in their heels and opt to continue their jumbled journeys through chaos for yet another year.

I understand that everyone needs to come to their own decisions, in their own time. And, I get the fact that change only comes about when one is ready. I can sure attest to that. I don't suggest or assume to know when another person's time has arrived. I get it. De-cluttering a house is a gargantuan task.

But when *I* get that call; when someone says, "I'm ready!" Watch out! Here comes the De-clutter Diva ... ... right at 'em!

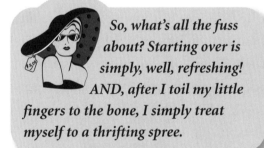

So, what's all the fuss about? Starting over is simply, well, refreshing! AND, after I toil my little fingers to the bone, I simply treat myself to a thrifting spree.

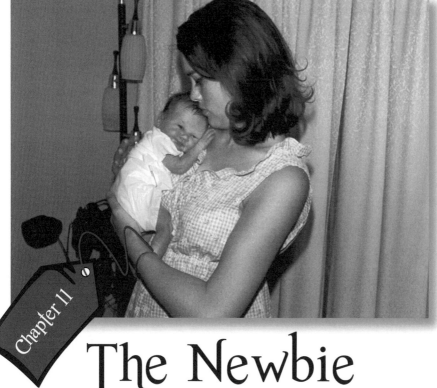

Chapter 11

The Newbie

ustomers who patronize retail stores have a veritable feast to choose from: price points, quality and specialty establishments. In other words, in the traditional retail space, there is practically a store for every budget or taste.

Most would agree that there is a world of difference between the merchandise offered at K Mart versus Neiman Marcus, yet both offer benefits for their customers.

Likewise, one can find a vast array of merchandise, from budget to high-end, at the numerous mom-and-pop tag sales held weekend after weekend on the driveways of America. It is for this reason that I disagree with the thrift gurus that strictly tout pricing merchandise cheaply.

Pricing is critical to the success of a yard sale. An ideal pricing structure makes money AND moves product.

While I agree with the premise that low prices move more product, I also think that type of strategy is too elementary. Determining the value of merchandise and tagging it with a fair sticker price is tricky, mainly due to the wide variety and condition of secondhand goods.

Training Wheels

I recently worked with a client who wanted to re-do her entire house. After living with things she didn't love for over 15 years, Jo was extremely excited to start the process. Her intent was to redecorate using thrift.

I had been down that road, many times. So we got busy putting my process to the test.

The first step involved a full-on purge of her home, ridding every cupboard and corner of clutter.

Furniture that was in dire need of replacement was hauled to the garage. Pictures were pulled off the walls and lamps were unplugged.

Then we set to the task of cleaning and tagging each item, the smallest of which were placed in storage boxes to await the upcoming garage sale, while the larger furniture was moved to the garage.

As we worked, Jo started to second guess herself; vacillating between keeping or tossing one doodad after another. That's when I put my Diva foot down … hard.

After agreeing to put my three-part questionnaire *(Do I love it, need it or can I buy it later?)* to the test, we de-cluttered her entire house, set up her garage like a boutique, and held her first Diva sale.

Now, we just might have to sit down and have a little "Come to Diva" chat.

The Diva-Sale

Jo was surprised at how attractive her merchandise looked once it was displayed, and we had to have another *Come to Diva* talk about not letting things drift back into her house. I simply did not want her to start second guessing her original decision to sell her unloved stuff.

What I knew, that she didn't, was that we would eventually embark on a grand journey; a shopping extravaganza to replace all her tired, old things with chic, frugal furnishings.

However, we were faced with one more challenge. Jo had little reference in determining how to price her sale items. She had some nice pieces that deserved a higher ticket ranging from $50 to $200; things like scuba gear, bicycles and exercise equipment.

Other items called for more restraint so we determined a mid-range spanning from $20 to $40.

And finally, there were items we just wanted to get rid of. Those were priced cheap; from $1 to $5. Our intent was to simply move them.

In the end we offered a range of levels; high-end, middle of the road, and cheap. There was something for everyone.

And it worked! Two hectic days later she was up $1,200!

Shopping for Thrift

Since that time, Jo has had a ball using her garage sale earnings to find amazing secondhand items to replace the worn and dated furnishings that she lived with for so long.

Once you get your "boutique" sale all set up, your castoffs are going to look so fab you'll be sorely tempted to sneak some things back into your house.

Now, if you even think about it . . . we're going to have another 'Come to Diva' meeting!

However, her biggest learning curve came when she realized that decorating with thrift was a challenge ... a creative process rather than an event. She learned that finding the things she loved took time and a hefty dollop of patience.

Things ran amuck when we tried to decorate her family room. Although we set out to furnish that room first, everything we found seemed to fit beautifully into her *living room.*

Jo quickly realized that thrift shopping was more like a toss of the dice ... never a sure thing.

She was used to the rifle approach—taking aim and firing. Conversely, she needed to take a shotgun approach when thrifting—taking in all the possibilities. The things she wanted or needed just didn't materialize ... right away. As a matter of fact, most of the things she fell in love with, and eventually bought, ended up in rooms other than her targeted areas.

The Armoire

One beautiful summer morning Jo and I ventured out to find an estate sale we had seen online. We pulled up to a small wood-frame house on the edge of downtown. After quickly surveying an uninteresting scattering of merchandise strewn across the driveway, we were ready to leave.

While Jo leafed through a box of records, I engaged the homeowner in a conversation about his sale. I asked if he had anything else we might look at. He mentioned an old armoire that was still in the basement, suggesting that it was simply too big to lug outside.

My ears perked up. After conferring with Jo, we confirmed that we wanted to take a look at it.

Following the man down a set of rickety steps, we entered a dank basement that housed the mighty antique; magnificent and alone.

I was smitten. I saw the potential of the old armoire immediately, but didn't want to confer with Jo in front of the seller. I guestimated that the piece would go for around $1000. However, I was hoping that the man would be very motivated to sell for two reasons; the relic was huge and I imagined he needed it out of the house. I nonchalantly questioned him a little more, then asked how much he was asking. He said he would be willing to let it go for $200. Wow, I knew that we had just stumbled upon a real deal, but I still didn't know if Jo wanted it. I needed to talk with her ... alone.

We climbed out of the basement and decided to walk around the sale for a bit. When we were out of ear-shot, I asked Jo if she liked the armoire.

"I love it!" she whispered. "But it's too big! How would I get it home?"

"Let me see what I can do." I left Jo and walked back to the owner.

"Look, we love the piece, but it is so big we're concerned about getting it home. We'll give you $150 if you help us load it into our truck and move it into her house."

I knew that I was pushing the envelope on this one, but without hesitation, the guy took me up on my offer.

Within a week that fabulous monster was nestled contentedly in the corner of Jo's living room.

Lessons Learned … the Easy Way

With each excursion into the fertile fields of thrift, Jo learned to make wise but quick decisions. She began to see the benefits of acting promptly whenever she found fabulous pieces at great prices … even if they were not exactly what she had in mind.

If she was undecided, I reminded her that she could always hold another sale the next year … and sell her mistakes. Over time her merchandise would increase in quality permitting her to command higher prices.

Just remember girlfriend, one Diva's mistake is another Diva's triumph!

Chapter 12

Smart Marketing ...

Big Payoffs

Whenever possible, my advertising efforts shout that I am running a high quality sale; one that hints at giving shoppers a chic, *Crate and Barrel* experience.

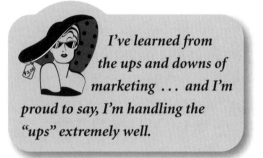

I've learned from the ups and downs of marketing ... and I'm proud to say, I'm handling the "ups" extremely well.

On the other hand, if a customer attends a sale from one of my roadside signs, they may not be prepared for the quality of the merchandise ... or the prices. So, I am prepared for a little fallout; people that make comments about my pricing or leave because they can't afford the merchandise.

However, I can and do use newspaper ads, Craigslist, *www.gsalr.com*, and *www.EstateSales.net* to inform potential customers of the type of event I am holding.

If I'm running a high-end sale, I work to attract customers who will appreciate the quality of my merchandise. On the other hand, if I just want to move product, I let them know that this is the sale for them ... chock full of budget-friendly deals.

Descriptive phrases tell a customer what to expect ... whether the merchandise falls in the bargain-basement category or discounted designer class.

A few of my favorite headliners include:
- *Everything Must Go!*
- *Let's Make a Deal!*
- *BARGAINS Galore!*
- *Prices Reduced Daily!*
- *Boutique Setting ... Garage Sale Prices.*

- *Fabulous Finds ... NO Junk!*
- *Decorator's Dream*
- *Designer Duds and Décor*
- *Amazing Sale ... Gorgeous Furnishings*
- *Posh SALE*
- *Cool stuff!*

Today, my intent is to attract the astute shopper. Therefore, my ads clearly indicate that I am holding a classy sale. Then, every attempt is made to create a chic environment; boutique-like arrangements, well-lit displays and clean merchandise.

In the end, my customers get more than they bargained for, which is why I have satisfied patrons that return year after year.

The Friendly Price Tag

If the intent of a seller is to simply move product, keep pricing low for the first sale or two. Additionally, if there are a lot of small ticket items like plastic containers, craft pieces, books, picture frames, or objects that are simply not in the best condition, it stands to reason that the merchandise will simply not warrant hefty prices.

The first time I ran a sale I learned a lot about pricing my merchandise. I had been thrifting for several years and I needed to get rid of a lot of stuff. Therefore, I sold a fair number of things for 50¢ or $1.00 while my better items ranged from $5 to $50.

I learned how to stage my sales to resemble a high-end boutique. Accordingly, my prices increased, as the quality of my merchandise improved.

Today, with an abundance of fine items to select from, I don't bother with the little stuff ... I just need to get rid of it. Usually, odds and ends get thrown into the *Free Box* ... a virtual goody package that is replenished regularly. This container magically divests the sale of all things that are simply not moving. By the end of the day, that carton is always empty, which minimizes the amount of stuff I have to haul to charity.

A Quality Decision

In the final analysis, I let the quality of my items determine my pricing. Inventory is marked to one-third of its retail cost. Therefore, if a brass fireplace set sells for $300 retail, I put a $99 price tag on it, assuming that it is still in great condition. If it is in fair condition, it might be priced from $10 to $50 accordingly.

It took me a while to understand that not all garage sales have to be clearance centers. There are plenty of people who are willing to pay $10 to $100 for unique décor or useful items,whereas, discriminating shoppers won't hesitate to pay $100 to $1000 for a special piece.

Darling, Trust me ... presentation is everything.

There is also an unsound fear that people will not attend a high-end garage sale. Or, if they do, they will refuse to come the next year. (I have not found this to be the case in the twenty-plus years I have been running my sales.) For me, if people decide to stay away, I contend that they are not the customer that I am trying to attract anyway.

In some instances, if I have a lot of first-rate merchandise to sell, I will advertise my sale as a *Living Estate Sale.* People simply know that they are apt to find better products at estate sales (whether someone has died or not) versus a yard sale.

One Woman's Trash is Another Woman's Treasure

A few years ago, I was selling a heap of wonderful designer clothes that I had priced between $10 and $50. During the sale I happened to be standing within hearing distance of two women examining my clothing. One exclaimed to no one in particular, "Geez, these prices are high." The other gal looked at her as if she were crazy. "Are you kidding?" she replied. "These are $200 to $300 designer clothes that are selling for $10 to $50!"

It was obvious that the first shopper didn't know the value of the clothes and was merely comparing my prices to other garage sales. The savvy shopper knew the value of the clothing and was ecstatic about the prices.

My point is this: it took some time, but eventually I began to understand my niche. Once I had a handle on who my customer was, I marketed specifically to that buyer. Today I offer quality merchandise at every sale, and I make between two and five thousand dollars a pop!

In addition, I've compiled a huge e-mail list of people who return year after year because they know they'll find great things at fair prices.

Pine Needle Creek

A very resourceful friend makes her home in the wilds of the Rocky Mountains, far from the hustle of the city. One would think that people would hesitate to drive the winding canyon roads to shop at her bi-yearly barn sale ... but they do!

Sonia decorates her charming mountain structure better than a high-end boutique and boasts a fabulous selection of furniture and household items that she has painstakingly collected throughout the garage sale season. People drive for miles to attend these enormously successful events.

For my part, I gather up my girlfriends, head up the mountain and make it a *girls only* outing. We gab, laugh and even get a chance to get some of our holiday shopping out of the way! Then we top the day off with a fabulous lunch and a soothing glass (or barrel) of our favorite wine.

Garage Sale Goals

Whenever I hold a sale, I give some thought to what I want to accomplish. If I simply want to get rid of things, I price items low, hoping to sell them quickly. If it is more important to realize a tidy profit while still moving my inventory, I assess my stock, sharpen my pencil just a bit, and make sure both goals are realized. With a well thought out system in place, people can find great merchandise and a darn good deal.

I am also a huge fan of specials. My ads let people know that on the first day, the merchandise sells at the sticker price. However, they are also getting the best selections. The second day boasts 25 percent off. And, the third day is *bargain day* at 50 to 75 percent off.

One might think that people might simply show up on the last day, but that is never the case. Shoppers arrive every day.

The first day satisfies the folks that are in search of quality items and unique finds.

The second day's 25 percent discount catches the people that might be hesitant to pay my Diva Sale prices.

And, the half-off event always brings in the crowd looking for the really big deals.

My guidelines for pricing inventory for a regular garage sale are as follows:

- **Books** – Books in good condition are priced at $1 for paperbacks and $3 for hardcover.
- **Clothing** – Children's clothing will sell at $1 to $3 and adult clothing, depending upon the condition, will fly off the racks at $3-$4.

   I put designer items on a separate rack and price them from $10 to $50. *Diva Tip: Clothing that is pressed and hung on hangers will sell for more than clothing thrown in a box sitting on a driveway.*
- **Electronics** – Electronics are hard to sell. Everyone is trying to get rid of them. I see bread makers, toasters, alarm clocks, CD players and coffee makers at every sale. When I sell appliances, I make sure they work, and price them from one-third to one-fourth of their retail value. If an item is still in the wrapper, I price it at 50 percent off its sticker price.

- **Toys** – Children's play things should be sold with caution. It is illegal to resell dangerous children's products since many have been recalled. So, sellers beware. If there are any questions regarding what and how to sell these items, spend some time researching the sale of used items on the Internet. There is a great site that offers a descriptive handbook on how to handle situations like this. Visit *www.cpsc.gov*, and then type in *Handbook for Resellers, Resale/Thrift Stores and Yard Sales.*

  Bag small toys together and sell them for $2. Bikes, ride-on toys, and large outside play equipment can bring $10 to $15 in good condition. Games, puzzles and everyday toys will sell at $1 to $3 if all the parts are there.

Many consumers and thrift store operators may be unaware of recalls, bans and current safety standards of products offered for sale in the stores.
~ Ann Brown

- **Furniture** – Furniture pieces, in good condition, move quickly. Everything is put through a reality check. If items are in poor condition, ripped, dented or scarred, they may not sell at all. If that's the case, I make a decision to give them away or price them at $10 or less, just to move them.

Then there are times I run a *Diva Sale* in order to make robust profits. I merchandize and price items in my *shoppe* with the discriminating buyer in mind. Antiques, designer pieces and unique discoveries are featured with artistic flair!

When advertising for this type of sale, I let people know that the event is high-end and more in line with estate sale pricing, thus my use of the promotional phrase ... *Living* Estate Sale.

Quality pieces will usually sell if I price them at one-third of their original retail price. Therefore, I always spiff up my merchandise by spot-cleaning soiled upholstery and adding a slick polish to any items. In other words, I work to display my furnishings to their best advantage.

At the same time that I am running my sale, I advertise my better pieces on Craigslist. If they do not sell, I will take them to a consignment shop to see if I can recoup some of my investment.

Chapter 13

Putting On The Glitz...

Selling used goods from a driveway, a yard, or the interior of a home has been referred to as a garage sale, yard sale, tag sale and on occasion, rummage sale. People hold these events to raise money or to simply get rid of unwanted items. Although they are a lot of work, holding a sale is a great way to de-clutter a home and turn used items into profits.

The following schedule outlines how I chunk down my tasks. With this approach, I find that the scope of my projects is seldom overwhelming.

A Diva of a Sale

Two Months Before the Garage Sale

I learned to set the dates of my sales by considering the financial mindset of a shopper. By scheduling my events around the 15th or 30th day of the month, I am more likely to hit a customer's payday. It stands to reason that people are more likely to splurge during those two days versus the times they walk around with no money in their pocketbooks. After all, my goal is to attract *buyers*, not *window shoppers*.

All my bags, boxes and paper goods that crept into my home were saved for the garage sale. By the time I opened my Diva Shoppe, I had collected a good stock of recycled wrappings to pack and box the items that I sold.

Two Weeks before the Sale

The transformation of my garage into the *Diva Shoppe* moves into high gear.

- Cars are pulled out. (If you are lucky enough to fit a car into your garage!)
- The entire area is prepped for the sale.
- Anything that is not being sold is moved to the back.
- Areas that will be off-limits are draped with sheets, thereby reducing a customer's temptation to examine items that are not for sale. This step is a huge time saver and prevents unnecessary distractions during the sale.
- The entire area is then cleaned from top to bottom.
- Next, display tables are set up in a U-shaped pattern, which allows for good traffic flow. People should be able to walk around and examine merchandise without tripping over things. In some instances, I place a row of tables down the middle if I need more surface area for displays.
- Every surface is then draped with sheets and topped with pretty tablecloths or pieces of fabric.
- My labeled boxes are hauled out and sorted by their contents, placing similar containers next to each other.

- I love to create scenes, so I place the same type of items, (*kitchen, family room, household, décor, clothing, toys*) in groupings so that I can arrange them quickly.
- My next project defines a *labor of love*. Tables are displayed with attention to detail. I go to great lengths to create eye-catching "tablescapes." My reason is simple ... people like to shop in attractive surroundings despite the fact that they are at a garage sale.

 *My recipe for a great Diva Sale is to add lots of creativity and a big dollop of sassy spice.*

- Furniture is arranged in scenes or quasi rooms. In turn, each area is festooned with accessories, throw pillows, pictures and silk plants to create a warm inviting designer look.

In the long run, the extra time and effort spent pulling together artful arrangements and furniture groupings results in heavier traffic and substantial sales.

One Week before the Sale

I have run sales in many states, some personal, and some for clients. Every locale has different requirements for holding sales and posting signs.

Check with the local authorities. Determine whether there are any garage sale ordinances or sign restrictions. (Some cities require a permit and stickers on all yard sale signs.)

I learned a hard lesson several years ago. I was holding a yard sale in Atlanta. People began arriving in droves. And, merchandise was flying out the door. Around noon, the sale came to a screeching halt. After closing down, I hopped in my car to check my signs. Every one had been taken down by the city. Although I corrected my blunder the next day, I lost the revenues of the first and busiest day.

Launch a hot marketing campaign.

- Watch for local competition. Nearby sales, rummage sales, flea markets, estate sales, thrift stores and auctions are great for pulling in more traffic which equates to increased sales.
- Advertisements should be placed in all the local newspapers. Most include online listings.
- Facebook, MySpace, Yahoo, Twitter and Google accounts should be peppered with your ads.
- Keep descriptions exciting and clear. People have many thrift choices ... especially in the thick of the garage sale season.
- Internet competition is stiff. Therefore, use enticing details. Listing centers like Craigslist have no limits on the amount of copy an advertiser can use, so advertise effusively ... more people will be lured to your sale.
- Copy should be edited as the sale progresses. Make it a point to list items that have sold. This has actually proven to entice more people to show up.

- New pictures, posted daily, take advantage of the statistics that prove pictures pull in 35 percent more viewers than ads without pictures.
- Craigslist is a very user-friendly site. Don't be afraid to play around with it to get your ads just right. Follow these five easy steps to load an ad:
  - Log into *www.Craigslist.com.*
  - On the right-hand side, see *Post* to *Classifieds.*
  - Write your ad copy and upload pictures of interesting and unique items.
  - Click the continue buttons until it says that an email will be sent confirming the advertisement. **Do not forget this step, or your copy will not be posted.**
  - Reply to the confirmation.

On the following page is a recent ad that I posted on Craigslist. Notice the abundant, playful copy that is used. Feel free to replicate any portion of the ad.

Two fabulous Divas are . . .

PUTTING ON THE GLITZ!

A "LIVING" ESTATE SALE

This funfilled, one-time event has two designer types
scurrying around emptying their coffers to bring you
fabulous items and great bargains.

Sorry guys, no tools or guns. This is a fabulous Diva SALE!

Join the fun! Everything is displayed indoors.
So, RAIN or SHINE, catch the great thrift wave!

FRIDAY-SATURDAY, OCTOBER 22-24, 9-4
3860 Clintbeck Way
Aurora, NE 68127

Check out the goodies:

- Kitchen items & small appliances: Two cooks ... too much of everything!
- Clothes: Designer Duds sizes 12-16
- Cool furniture: Antique & Vintage
- Lots of décor: Lamps, table accessories, plant stands, throw pillows, rugs
- Boudoir: lovely bedding, bed throws, pillows
- Beautiful glassware and colorful dishware
- Lots more to list but my arm is cramping up ... please join us!

Garage Sale signs are critical to the success of a sale. I whip up a mess of vibrant, eye-catching signs, and post them legally, separate from other tag sale advertising.

- Make signs BOLD and easy to read from a passing car.
- Check your signs frequently to make sure they stay posted for the entire length of the sale.
- Put your advertising on foam board ... not construction paper!
- Wording should be short and powerful. These are a few of my favorite postings (depending on the type of sale I am running):
  - **DESIGNER GARAGE SALE**
  - **"LIVING" ESTATE SALE**
  - **BARGAIN YARD SALE**
- Avoid words like *huge, big,* or *multifamily.* I have been to sales that advertise more merchandise than IKEA. Curious, I've trudged through rain and hail only to find a paltry amount of merchandise. From experience, I simply don't trust that type of advertising.

- Signs should be BIG and SIMPLE.
- Forget about adding addresses to your postings. Instead, use a BIG ARROW to point customers in the right direction.
- Make all arrows the same color so customers know they are on the right track.
- PRINT ALL SIGNS.
- Separate yourself from the pack; place signage far from the signs others have posted.

Signs that catch my attention and take me right to the doorstep of a tag sale are my delight. I have found real bargain bins that weren't even on my list because someone made the effort to post effective signage—signs that were easy to read and told me exactly where to go.

I also post my sales on Internet sites that allow *free* postings.

www.Garage-Sale-Tips-Maps.com
www.gsalr.com
www.WeekendTreasure.com
www.GarageSaleHunter.com
www.YardsaleAD.com
www.ClassifiedAds.com
www.kijiji.com

Garage Sale signs should be SIMPLE and EASY TO READ.

The Day Before the Sale

There is always a lot to do right before I open for business. If I don't have everything done ... I'm stuck. I can't leave the sale to run to the store, or the bank, or to put out more signs. So the day before all hell breaks loose, I undertake my last-minute preparations.

A trip to the bank is the first item on my agenda. I pick up a minimum of $100 in small bills. At the least, I make sure I have fifty $1's, six $5's and two $10's. I've learned that people will often hand you a $20 bill to pay for a $3 item because they have come straight from their bank or ATM machine.

Garage sale signs are put out the day before the sale. By placing my advertising at strategic corners at 4:00 p.m. (drive time), I catch an extra day of free promotion. The next morning I do an early morning drive-by to make sure that all the signs are still up.

Electrical outlets are placed in convenient locations. This convenience and allows shoppers the opportunity to test their electrical items. A sign that reads, TEST APPLIANCES HERE, is hung next to each outlet.

My neighbors receive a courtesy call. Each is invited over and offered a 30 percent discount. They always appreciate my thoughtfulness. I have also found that they become great customers and have even added their castoffs to my sale.

Two card tables are set up between the garage and the outside. I use one for check out and the other for holding items.

The **CHECKOUT TABLE** serves as a worktable where merchandise can be re-tagged, dirty inventory cleaned and people can pay for their purchases. I also store my supplies on the checkout table in a handy organizer that includes:

- Calculator
- Markers
- Pens
- Tape measure
- Hammer and nails
- Tape
- Scissors
- Price tags

I have a handy little organizer that I use as well. I simply ask him his availability and pencil him in.

- Recycled packing material
- Pad of paper
- A supply of business cards
- Email sign-up sheet (for my next sale)
- Jewelry and expensive items
- Batteries to test appliances and toys
- Personal items (phone, water, food in a cooler)
- A large supply of aspirin (just kidding)
- Makeup (not kidding)

The **HOLD TABLE** is a place where people can safely store things while they continue to shop without fear of someone buying their treasures. This table should be kept empty except for a large HOLD TABLE sign that is attached, in plain sight.

This convenient table is critical for making multiple sales. Clients tend to pass up merchandise that they are unable to examine, and they like to inspect the things they are considering. A HOLD Table provides a safe place for them to stow their items, which usually equates to more sales.

Instead of serving candy at my sales, I prefer a little 'eye-candy' standing next to my HOLD table. I simply think it's good for business.

The HOLD TABLE also allows the seller to note the types of things a customer is buying. This is a perfect opportunity to guide shoppers to other items that might pique their interest.

Sale Day!

When the big day arrives, I still have much to do. I usually rise at 4:00 a.m., shower, put on full makeup, dress in a chic outfit, snap my fanny pack on and head out to the garage by 5:00 a.m. (After all, I am the proprietress of this amazing Diva Shoppe and I love to dress the part!) As I open the sale, I'm reminded that there will be early shoppers.

- All lamps are turned on. I display an assortment of lamps because light attracts people and makes the boutique look warm and inviting.
- Cars are moved down the block. Parking always seems to be at a premium so I open up as many parking spaces as possible.
- Several large, attractive pieces of furniture are dragged down toward the curb. I find that some people do drive-bys to see if the sale is worth their time. Busy shoppers don't want to waste time stopping at meager sales. By placing enticing items near the curbside, hesitant shoppers are encouraged to stop and shop.
- All doors are locked including the door from the garage into the house. If I have to enter my home during the sale I get out my key, open it and lock it behind me.
- A FREE box is placed near the front of the sale. Throughout the sale, it's filled with things that aren't selling. (Tip: I even throw in broken or chipped articles because some people are very resourceful and good at repairing wounded items. If the box isn't empty by the end of each day, the contents are tossed or place at the curb for some lucky recipient.)

I'm always on the lookout for dead spots; areas that people keep passing over. Sometimes a particular corner or dark area is simply lifeless. Garage sales have dead spots just like retail stores, so if I see items that are constantly being overlooked, I move them. My motto: If it's not selling … re-arrange it.

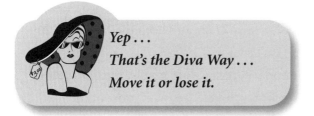

Yep ...
That's the Diva Way ...
Move it or lose it.

- All clothes are hung on hangers and displayed on a clothes rack or a makeshift area formed by a shower rod placed between two ladders.
- A checkout table is then positioned at the opening to the garage. This allows me to keep tabs on what is going on inside the garage as well as the merchandise on the driveway.
- A patio umbrella or a tent over the checkout table serves as a welcome relief in the summer months, and protects my valuables from too much sun or a damaging sprinkle.
- My money is kept in a fanny-pack attached to my waist, allowing for freedom of movement without leaving a cashbox unattended.

Trust me ... this Diva
NEVER lets any form of
BLING out of her sight.

- Serious buyers and dealers typically arrive an hour or so before the sale opens. I welcome them. They are typically good customers and readily pay for what they want.
- Friends and partners are asked to arrive an hour before the sale ... ready to work; two hours before if they have things to set up.

- My mission is to get rid of everything. As the sale progresses, I reduce prices, negotiate like crazy and keep the FREE box full of merchandise that isn't selling.
- An upbeat attitude and a party face are irresistible. People love shopping in a festive atmosphere. And, with most of the hard word behind me ... it's easy to have fun.
- At the end of the sale, I stick to my guns, making sure I don't relent and allow a favored item to sneak back into my house.

Did someone say "party?"

- Then I separate what I need to store for the next sale and what will be donated.
- My car is packed with the merchandise that is going to my preferred charities, buy myself a big latte and revel in a job well done.
- I make a list of everything I am donating, and assign a value to each item. I then attach the list to the signed receipt I get from the drop-off center.
- Typical categories used for tax purposes:
  Clothing
  Shoes
  Linens
  Small Furniture
  Sporting Equipment
  Toys
  Décor and Household
  Jewelry
  Books
  Appliances

A BIG sale can be a boom or a bust. However, with some thoughtful planning, you can make it a great success. Go with the flow … meet interesting people and have fun. Make it a fabulous Diva Day to remember!

 text: Chapter 14

Living with a Diva

My husband hates, I mean really detests, anything that has to do with the thrift scene. I would imagine he feels that way because the act of thrifting is not a neat and tidy process. Nor is it predictable. The hunt holds little infatuation for this pragmatic man, and he sees no sense in pursuing the unknown. His approach to shopping is simple: determine what is needed, find the best price, locate the item and buy it.

On occasion his resolve gives way when I come home with a bargain. Last summer he mentioned in passing that he needed a mower which I promptly found at a garage sale for fifty bucks ... brand new.

The mower was something he needed, the price met with his frugal nature, and I did all the schlepping, delivering it neatly to our front door.

Now, that's the way he likes to thrift shop.

The Flea Market

This past summer I roped him into helping me run a booth at one of the local flea markets. Although he was able to maintain a degree of resigned helpfulness throughout most of the sale, he couldn't hide his sheer and utter boredom toward the end of one particularly hot and sultry afternoon.

Turning from a customer who had just bought a vintage teapot, I noticed that my macho mountain man was nonchalantly sitting at the checkout table with a square container affixed to his head. Of course, I had to laugh and snap a picture, but I also got the message: *I really don't like doing this.*

Unless I'm making money from my thrifting passion, as do professional decorators, thrift writers, and radio or TV personalities like Leigh and Leslie Keno, I don't really expect much more than a perfunctory nod from my spouse or family. I've learned to accept the stony silences that greet me whenever I regale them with my thrifting adventures.

In talking with other frugal, creative women, I've come to realize that most significant others are just not interested or appreciative of their spouse's time and efforts. Most just shake their heads, thinking we've lost our marbles, and go off to play with *their* toys. Ah, ya just gotta love 'em!

The Fashionista

Chapter 15

People often ask me if I buy secondhand clothes. I usually give them a devious smile that says, "Of course I do, and I probably pay a whole lot less for my stuff than you do for yours."

Now I understand that everyone has their own level of comfort, but the way I figure it, if I can wash it, I can wear it.

Shhh ... I do wear thrift. And, I must say ... I simply look marvelous!

What is Divawear?

Years ago I began referring to my clothing as Divawear. Granted, it is a very cheeky term, but I love its panache. It carries a certain flourish and announces my personal style.

Whenever I shop with my girlfriends they invariably pull a piece of glitz off the rack, hold it up, and with complete conviction say, "Barb, this is so you." What they are saying is that I have created a signature look, a style that represents my persona—my Divaness.

Divawear is fun ... a fashion sense that doesn't take itself too seriously.

Most people don't realize that they are telegraphing their "image" to everyone they meet.

~~~

*That was it. Suddenly you hit puberty, and it's like,
you know, thrift stores! I just started deconstructing
everything from thrift stores.*
~ Gwen Stefani

~~~

The great news is that we women aren't thrown-into the mono-chromatic abyss. We don't have to dress in suits in varying shades black, grey or blue. We are peacocks! We can have a good time with our fashion sense while taking delight in our Diva ways.

The way I dress announces … I am fantastic. Come hang with me. Get to know me. I am fun. I am playful. I am victorious. I am a Diva.

Delicious Savings

Divawear doesn't cost a fortune, but it looks fabulous. Many of my better pieces come from stores that specialize in vintage. I haunt estate sales and consignment shops as they often carry designer or couture fashions.

In addition, I intersperse older pieces with new; accessories and thoughtful gifts from friends.

I operate like a search beacon; always on the lookout for unique pieces that might pop up during the special sales at my preferred thrift venues.

Recently, while shopping at my preferred DAV store on their 99¢ day, I ran across this fabulous 50's coat. I snatched that baby up just in time for the holidays. This picture was taken of me in my 99¢ *find*, right before I went out with my handsome husband. I was simply feeling way too glam!

The Diva Exchange

Exchanging or giving clothes to my girlfriends is a kick. I wish I could say that my generosity is due to my charitable nature, but the truth of the matters is, I simply don't fit into many of my fabulous finds any longer.

At this stage in my life I figure the only chance I have of getting back into shape is if I'm asked to be a contestant on *Dancing with the Stars*.

I might not win the dance competition on Dancing with the Stars, *but who cares... have you seen those buff dancers? Check... them... out!*

I would venture to say that the chances of that happening are pretty slim, so it appears I'll just have to keep shopping and purging as my sizes fluctuate.

My glorious Michigan Divafriends are not only very stylish, but they have a zest for life that is magnetic. We've been hanging together for years, and they love to attend my garage sales as well as my clothing exchanges.

Once a year I give tons of Divawear away when they visit me in Colorado for our annual ski trip.

Last year I asked them to pack light. Upon their arrival I presented them with garbage bags full of ski outfits and all the bling they could stuff into their suitcases.

A Diva Wedding

Another Divaesque moment occurred the night before my wedding in the quaint village of Aspen, Colorado. Stephen and I received a fabulous gift; a magnificent western party, thrown by a dear family friend. Invitations to the rehearsal "party" were sent out suggesting that the guests dress in western attire. Needless to say my girlfriends showed up all decked out in the most fabulous western finery, which, I might add, decidedly outshone the bride.

These Diva-pals are as spirited as they are talented, and we have hung together through 20 years of marriages, divorces, business startups and downturns in the economy ... all of which cemented our friendships and strengthened our mettle.

The Never End

Chapter 16

People often ask why I refer to myself as a Diva. Well, that's probably a whole other book. However, I do owe you a brief explanation.

The Warrior Within

When I was growing up in the fifties and sixties, I was caught between two ambiguous eras where strong female role models were emerging, and the movement toward a more independent, self-actualized woman was starting to percolate.

Although the trend was reflected in the fashions of the day, the consciousness of women was brought to light by the ever-progressive motion picture industry. Here, among the drawing boards and fabric bolts of Hollywood design studios, life began to imitate art when Marlene Dietrich created a furor wearing pants in the 1930s film *Morocco*. Garbo soon followed suit, and the rest was another cornerstone in female history.

But the Diva who really touched my soul was Katherine Hepburn. Throughout her film career, Kate maintained her fierce independence, took full ownership of her controversial label, and was quick to challenge convention. Most of all, she loathed labels and inequity.

When asked, in an NBC interview, why she wore pants the outspoken actor proclaimed,

I just had good timing. The times fit me. Pants came in, low heels came in, and the terrible woman came in...who spoke her mind.

Kate extolled, with feisty abandon, her beliefs in education, human sexuality and birth control, and applauded women's rights. Katherine Hepburn was a Diva. A warrior. A woman who savored the moment and danced to her own beat.

Although growing up in the shadows was the norm for women of my generation, strong, vibrant and daring females continued to emerge. Jacqueline Kennedy epitomized the strength of the sixties woman and was indeed a soldier in both fashion and fact. Gloria Steinem, despised and revered, was and is an unquestionable testament to the pursuit of the feminine.

These amazing women were just a few of the many role models that nudged me away from the security of a predictable life and comforts of a mundane existence.

During those exciting, turbulent years, women burned their bras as a symbol of a female society unwilling to be harnessed to an outdated plow. And, the movie industry awakened my restless passions as I passed from the spring of my youth into the summer of my adolescence.

Still today, movies like *Beaches* and *Steel Magnolias* are apologetically referred to as "chick flicks," ignoring or diminishing the power of their titles or the mettle of their characters. To me, these films capture the Diva character, embracing and intertwining the beguiling spirit of the feminine with the resolve of the warrior.

A Warrior's Mission

It saddens me to realize that our society has, to this point, typically honored only the heroes of the battlefields or boardrooms.

I believe that women are heroes. They guard the sick and forlorn; shape the pages of children's storybooks; and work the factories when men go to war. These silent warriors are the stalwart souls who guarded the gates to the underground railroads, crisscrossing the centuries with their tears.

Yesterday, women sheltered the persecuted; today, they protect the abused. In the past, they entered the male dominated bastions of management; today, they are breaking glass ceilings at unprecedented rates.

Divas are indeed heroic. They stand tall and fight for their beliefs. Marching through time in all shapes, sizes and ages, they fan the flames of their obsessions and ignite their passions . . . their careers, families, social commitments and philanthropic projects.

Some women find their paths early and lead rich, full lives while others discover their missions later in life, reveling in newly-found bliss.

Viking Runes

In reflecting on each unique and individual journey, I am reminded of the Viking runes. Their smooth and ancient hieroglyphics are said to foretell one's cosmic direction.

Out of 27 fortuitous symbols there is one stone that remains blank. Although disquieting at first, it is the most powerful and promising of the runes contained within their prophetic pouch.

The *naked* rune is far from bare. It is said to be the pregnant stone ... the harbinger of all possibilities.

If one is lucky enough to chose this rune, it is said that she has the opportunity to harness the power of the unknown; the courage and faith necessary to step into the void and claim the Diva warrior within.

The Thrift Journey

Becoming a *Thrift Diva* is a heady experience. Some treasure hunters have attained the designation from years of patient searching. Others have benefited from the meticulous mentoring of wise thrift practitioners befriended while bumping heads at some frenzied sale.

Regardless of how they attained their status, these thrifty warriors are the loyalists that can be found patiently queuing up long before the doors open, welcoming them to another round of *thrift mania.*

Katherine Hepburn, that grand Diva, once remarked, "If you always do what interests you, at least one person is pleased."

Meanwhile, other adventurers continue to stop by roadside hoards rescuing relics tossed aside by hasty hands.

Thrifters arrive in varying guises; blissfully hooked on their passions ... ignoring the peaks and valleys of their quests.

Some work tirelessly to create beautiful, serene homes for their families while others strive to carve out tastefully decorated dwellings—at little to no cost.

I am inspired by those ambitious soldiers who embrace their entrepreneurial leanings, roll up their sleeves and open their own thrift stores or consignment shops.

Regardless of where our journeys end ... or if they ever do, the adventurous continue to march into the world of thrift, and find that their frugal stages are set with twists and intrigue.

Just rewards are rightfully earned by fervent thrifters who ignore the inconveniences that routinely halt the meek and hesitant. These stalwart souls forge onward, lured by the promises of reclaimed treasures.

The rite of passage is only granted to the hardy; those with a thirst for the unusual and tough enough to risk the ridicule of those who frequent more elegant venues.

Thrifting is a perfect outlet for the daring—those enterprising souls that triumph over sordid back-alley thrift stores and the gloomy recesses of neighborhood garage sales.

But *Thrift Divas* are more than collectors of backyard trash, they are the plucky spirits that find the magic in the mundane, inspire the less fortunate and use their creative genius to build their own castles.

The Never End

Appendix
Resources, Deals, and Tips

America is having a love affair with thrift. The green movement has turned selling used goods into big business. With a downturn in the economy, people are catching on to the huge savings that the thrift venues offer.

The halls of thrift are not, as some erroneously imagine, solely patronized by the unemployed or impoverished. People from all walks of life have been spotted streaming into their local resale stores or rummaging through the second-hand goodies at garage sales and flea markets. Patrons range from young adults dressing retro and decorating their apartments in *Shabby Chic,* to boomers living on fixed budgets, and outfitting their retirement homes.

In addition, this timely trend boasts a broad range of collectors and thrift aficionados. These enthusiasts comb the loaded bargain bins to resell their finds on eBay or Craigslist, or at their local flea markets.

I have accumulated a host of information from years spent searching the Internet and scouring through thrift shops, consignment stores, and antique malls as I crisscrossed the nation on my thrifting journies. My hope is that the reader finds the list of resources and blog sites timely and supportive.

National Thrift Organizations

The National Association of Resale and Thrift Shops (NARTS), *www.NARTS.org,* is the best resource for consignment, resale, and thrift store information. It is a qualified organization that trains and supports people within the thrift industry. This site has a wealth of information essential for starting and operating a resale shop, as well as resources for educational books, tips, and a calendar of events.

Nonprofit Thrift Store Chains

A great online resource for locating thrift stores in any state is *www.TheThriftShopper.com*. In addition to having a directory for thrift shops by area, it offers a heady supply of thrift tips and procedures.

Spread across the country, in ever increasing numbers, are a series of attractive, well stocked thrift store chains:

The DAV (Disabled American Veterans) Chain, *www.DAV.org*

Founded in 1920 for those afflicted in World War I, this charity has become the voice of the nation's disabled wartime veterans and their families.

Peppered across the United States, DAV offers great promotional sales. Check in your area for promotional savings and events.

Many stores color-code their inventory. In my home state, Mondays are clearance days, offering one color that is 99¢, excluding furniture. There are tremendous bargains to be had for a buck in clothing, lamps, art, tools, décor and linens. People line up 15 minutes before the doors open, and dealers and homemakers alike expectantly queue for great deals.

The Goodwill Stores Chain, *www.Goodwill.org*

Goodwill is one of several national and international thrift chains that offer a thrift environment with strong corporate leadership, making the operations of this retail system consistent throughout the country.

Like most stores that market secondhand goods, Goodwill offers a variety of used products and promotes weekly and monthly specials. On a weekly basis, one color is offered at 50 percent off. Once a month the chain runs a storewide 50 percent off special. This is a great way to get thrift merchandise at even lower prices.

Salvation Army Thrift Stores Chain, *www.SalvationArmyUSA.org*
The Salvation Army, founded in Great Britain in 1865, started as a religious movement with a focus on social and charitable work. Today the retail stores pepper the United States, still supporting the poor, the destitute and the hungry.

The stores are well lit, nicely displayed and typically run holiday and weekly specials.

St. Vincent de Paul Thrift Store Chain, *www.SVDPUSA.org*
Like most thrift chains, St. Vincent de Paul operates a string of thrift stores, the proceeds of which support the Society's mission to serve the poor and indigent. Below is a list of just a few of St. Vincent de Paul's assistance programs.

- Emergency financial assistance
- Food programs and disaster relief
- Rent and mortgage assistance/Low-cost housing
- Shelters for the homeless and abused
- Employment services/Job training
- Education programs (GED)
- Youth programs/Camp programs

The Arc Thrift Store Chain, *www.ArcThrift.com*

The Arc Thrift Stores are a Colorado-based chain offering many services and monthly specials:

Sun	Mon	Tues	Wed	Thurs	Fri	Sat
			1	2	3	4 50% off SALE!
5	6	7 Seniors' Day 50% Off	8	9	10	11 50% off SALE!
12	13	14 Seniors' Day 50% Off	15	16	17	18 50% off SALE!
19	20	21 Seniors' Day 50% Off	22	23	24	25 50% off SALE!
26	27	28 Seniors' Day 50% Off				

In addition, the chain offers the following services to assist individuals within the community:

- Educating legislators
- Advocacy for children and adults
- Vocational and housing services
- Community organizing and public awareness

For-profit Thrift Store Chains

There are many mom and pop for-profit thrift stores scattered throughout cities and towns across the nation. However, *Savers* is one of the few major *for-profit* chains.

Savers, *www.Savers.com*

Launched in 1954, this for-profit thrift enterprise operates in the United States under the trade names *Savers* and *Value Village,* and in Canada it is known as the *Value Village Store.* It is the largest *for-profit* thrift store chain internationally.

How to Locate Estate Sales

When I am deep in the throes of the thrifting season, I attend as many estate sales as possible and always ask to be put on a company's mailing list. These notices keep me apprised of all upcoming events.

I also search the Internet to find nearby sales. *www.EstateSales.net* is an online site that locates estate sales, tag sales, and auctions in any given area. By clicking on the desired state (on the U.S. map) the user is quickly directed to that state. Clicking further will take the user into a designated town.

How to Find a Consignment Shop

Locally owned and run consignment shops can be found scattered throughout the towns and burgs across America. There are several on-line sites that list consignment shops by state:

www.ConsignmentShops.com
www.ConsignmentPal.com
www.HowToConsign.com

Friendly Craigslist

Craigslist, *www.craigslist.com*, is one of my favorite resources. Not only do I scour this site regularly for sales, I also post my personal garage sales as well as my famous *Living Estate Sales.*

This enterprising Internet listing system was started in 1995 by Craig Newmark in the San Francisco Bay area. By 2007, Craigslist had established itself in approximately 450 cities in 50 countries. Here's the kicker ... the site's sole source of revenue is *job ads.* It gets a whopping nine billion page views a month. The good news for us thrift seekers is the garage sale, estate sale, and yard sale ad portion is free!

Easy eBay

I have never sold much on EBay, *www.eBay.com,* specifically because I have focused and enjoyed the hands-on, belly-to-belly repartee that garage sales, flea markets and estate sales offer. However, that doesn't mean that a tidy profit can't be had. The key to making money is all about how much an item is *bought* for versus what it is *sold* for. A good guide for buying the right things to sell on eBay is *The eBay Seller's Guide to Finding Profitable Hidden Bargains at Garage Sales* by Robbin K. Tungett.

Scary Auctions

Auctions, *www.AuctionsZip.com,* offer a wide variety of products for those who want to explore the fast pace of the bidding world. Click on this site and enter a zip code; select the maximum distance you are willing to drive; and *Voila!* ... a calendar with all the local auctions will appear.

Diva Tip: For those eBay aficionados that find their low bids pulled out from under them at the last minute, try this nifty site: *www.AuctionSniper.com.*

Locating and Mapping Sales on the Internet

www.gsalr.com

Hands down, this site is my favorite place for locating and mapping local garage sales, yard sales, tag sales and estate sales.

www.TheThriftShopper.com

Although this is a great resource for finding local thrift stores and links to other thrift related sites, it also contains thrifting tips and frugal shopping maneuvers.

www.AreaGuides.net

Simply enter the city, then the venue (thrift stores, antique or consignment shops) and ... presto, the resale establishments in any given area line up.

www.GarageSalesTracker.com

Find a sale, post a sale, blog, print coupons, locate consignment shops and flea markets, and read garage sale tips under this site designed for both shoppers and sellers.

www.YardSalePortal.com

Along with thrifty tips for online buying and selling, this location offers the opportunity to advertise yard or garage sales, sell online, and search to find tag sales, garage sales, estate sales, or yard sales in a variety of states.

Motivation, Leadership, and Inspiration

I have sought inspiration in varying levels, at various times. I discovered that a rich tapestry of inspired messages awaits the seeker. These insights arrive in many forms: a song heard in the background, a headline, a book title. Perhaps the universe is calling, vying for attention.

Regardless of the venue or purpose of these whisperings, I believe that a connection with a higher power is occurring.

The following sites not only inspire, but allow women to connect with one another; women from all walks of life; promoting businesses, sharing information and creating blogs.

Here are some of my personal favorites:

- For women who choose to be "Inspiration in Action", check out *www.BraveHeartWomen.com.*
- If women, health, family, love, beauty, and entertainment are of interest to you, www.*WomenOnlyBlogs.com* is a great resource.
- To read or start a blog on women's issues; *http://en.wordpress.com/tag/womens-issues/*
- I love that this site is celebrating women...50 and better; *www.FeistySideOfFifty.com.*
- *www.DivaTribe.com* is a community of strength, support and creativity for women.
- Empowerment, inspiration, connection and success is the mantra for *www.newerawomen.ning.com.*

E-Zine Magazines

Holding Thrift is an online magazine that offers advice and what is happening on the thrift scene. Check out *wwwTheNationalThrifter.com.*

Swap Meets

Swapping has become a national rage. My girlfriends and I have been trading things for years. So if you love parties and want some new-to-you fashions, invite some friends and do a clothing exchange. If you are into books, video games or CDs, check out *www.SwapTree.com.*

Common Thrift Terms and Thrifty Tips

Terms

Thrift – A broad generic term comprised of secondhand goods sold at garage sales, tag sales, yard sales, thrift stores, rummage sales, estate sales, antique shops, consignment stores, flea markets and auctions.

Thrifters – A group of stalwart treasure seekers who are hopelessly hooked on their passions, blindly ignoring the peaks and valleys of their frugal quests.

Resale, Secondhand, Used, Gently Used, Thrift, Castoffs, Junk – Describes used items that a person has thrown out, handed down, sold or donated.

Vintage – Typically refers to items from 50 to 99 years. However, vintage *apparel* spans from the Victorian styles of the 1800's to the disco craze of the 1970's.

Antique – Clothing and furnishings that are 100 years or more are classified as antique.

Consignment – Quality clothing and furnishings, in good condition, which are sold through a consignor who shares the proceeds of a sale.

A Happy Camper – A warrior Diva who, against all odds, becomes a frugal fashionista and decorates her home with artistic flair and individuality with secondhand or shabby chic items … at little to no cost.

Dumpster Diver – A salvager of used goods found in dumpsters.

Road-kill – Items left at the side of the road, free for the taking … typically, but not solely, put out on trash day.

Swap Meet – An exchange or *swapping* of clothing and furnishings.

Thrifty Tips

Find a favorite thrift venue – Use the yellow pages, Internet, library and referrals to locate a thrift venue that fits your needs ... and budget.

Go for the gold – It takes awhile to develop a trained eye. In the beginning buy things you love, and avoid buying just because it's a great deal.

Check and recheck – Check secondhand items for quality and flaws; flaws can often be repaired ... quality can't.

Be patient – Thrift shopping offers great deals and incredible products, but the very things you are looking for may not show up for months.

Out with the old – A yearly purge is cathartic. Get rid of everything you don't need, love or use.

Buy cautiously; spend wisely – Saving money by buying thrift is great ... spending *found* money (from a purge) is even better!

Get your feet wet – Dip your toes into the thrift pool by finding a fabulous secondhand piece ... it's addictive!

When in doubt – Don't turn down those fabulous finds! If space is a problem ... start purging!

Practice makes perfect – Buying, selling and decorating with thrift is an art; it takes patience and practice.

Make no mistake – Turn your thrifting *mistakes* into cash. Commit to holding a yearly garage sale and selling items that no longer work ... or never did!

Rule of thumb – Thrift shopping can save a thrifter between 50 to 80 percent off retail price.

Buy off season – Take a cue from retail; shop thrift venues that flush out their off-season, deeply discounted merchandise.

Put on a *Diva* sale – Turn dreary garage sales into *Diva Boutiques*; replete with clean merchandise, "quasi" rooms, beautiful *tablescapes*, and hot ad campaigns.

The FREE box – Purge yard sales of *slow movers*! Create a FREE box for items that don't sell or are not worth the bother.

Don't fret the small stuff – Dealing with change, nickels and dimes, is not worth the effort. Toss cheap items into the FREE Box or bundle them into $1.00 bags.

Timing the Deal – Shop *early* to find unique items — shop *late* to get the deals.

Be GREEN and Generous – Recycle your household items by donating all unloved, unused and unnecessary *stuff* to your favorite charity ... yearly.

Create a Thrifting Map – Use the Internet to find and map garage sales and estate sales before forging into the *jungles of junk*.

Buy a GPS system – This Geo tracker saves thrifters' time and their sanity! Seriously, I wouldn't leave home without mine!

Have FUN – Treasure every moment of every day. Happy hunting!

Chapter from Barb's next book ...

Tossed and Turned

... Decorating with the Thrift Diva

The Diva Lair

Ancient rites call, awakening the creative powers that have coursed through our veins since the beginning of time; harkening the timeless call to gather and nest.

Despite the flow of generations, the same primal drives that prompted the wall paintings of the cave dwellers continue to influence us today as we make our marks on the signature lines of our homes.

Aside from the visual and spiritual enjoyment of harmonious spaces, most women need to create a place that is specifically theirs; a spot that is more personal than the other rooms in their homes ... an area

that is theirs alone. A place that awakens the Diva within. A sanctuary that is as liberating as it is individual. A haven where spirit is celebrated and energies renewed. A shield against the daily chaos . . . if only for a moment.

Staking Claim

The size of the space is irrelevant. It can be an entire house or a nook nestled in a remote room. Some women etch their signatures on every facet of their homes; simple exquisite touches that delight the soul. Others carve out their niches in dens or studies, in craft rooms and basements.

Creating a Diva spot is infinitely affordable. After all, what price can be put on harmony? Inner peace? Acknowledgement? Validation? Or, delight?

I have a friend whose husband built an entire barn for her. She loves collecting antiques and refurbishing the tarnished treasures she gathers.

Nine months out of the year the space is a workshop where she sorts, and mends and paints, delighting in the restoration of the orphaned castoffs she has collected throughout the year with methodical intensity.

This artist works for weeks transforming her barn into a virtual fairytale boutique. Then, magically, twice a year, she opens it for two spectacular events; an October Extravaganza and a Holiday Affair.

Veteran and beginning treasure seekers alike travel great distances through craggy mountain passes to attend Sonia's gala events; the culmination of her thrifting excursions and a testament to her artistry.

couture

Penny-pinching Couture

In my own home I have created a "Diva Dressing Room" which lives in stark contrast to the rough beauty of mountain living. This uniquely personal haven was carved from a former bedroom. Its walls shelter my daywear, evening attire, bobbles and jewelry and even a delicious dabbling of *Sex in the City* shoes.

Within these hallowed walls I am surrounded by things of beauty; items collected over the years from consignment stores, thrift shops, estate sales, auctions, garage sales, yard sales and tag sales. Clothes and baubles, reminiscent of bygone eras, hang from every corner. Nooks and shelves are festooned with vintage creations that greet me whenever I enter this intimate space.

Delicate scents, in old Avon bottles, grace every projection, filled with the sweet fragrances of yesteryear. These evocative perfumes, discovered within the dusty coffers of the thrift world, are sprayed just as frequently as my signature perfume, Pheromone.

A simple splash of these reminiscent mists transport me back to the 50s and 60s

and the old farm table where my mother and I poured over Avon catalogs, always choosing, despite the vast array of new scents, Topaz and Cotillion, the most evocative and wistful of the old bouquets.

Scarves of all weaves and lengths hang from scattered hooks, ready to be claimed at the last minute, adding their autograph to the outfit of the day. These lively strands of color, like most vestiges that hang within this glitz-filled haven, have been lovingly collected from various frugal concerns.

Peppered amongst the regulars are a smattering of out-of-season finds and a collection of handy gifts ready to be wrapped and presented to a thoughtful hostess or girlfriend celebrating a rite of passage.

Discovering the Magic

On a deeper level, women don't always take care of their needs. However difficult the balancing act may be, the caretakers of this planet need to care for themselves as much as they do for others, restoring the natural balance of the earth.

Women are the glue in the universe. They need to embrace their magic, believe in their power and celebrate their contributions to this planet. As Martha Stewart says, "It's a good thing."

Challenges from Within

We will always be tested. At times a spouse may not support our efforts, acquaintances will scoff at our drives and ambitions; there will be

downturns in the economy, childlessness—or unexpected children—job demands or the loss of employment. The list is endless. It is no wonder that years pass while we and our homes remain the same . . . shabby and uninspiring.

We may rage over our fate when resources are scarce or support systems fail, but too often, when we feel the most vulnerable, we let resignation reign.

Challenges will always arrive, unfettered. Left to their device these thieves of harmony can dishearten us and leave us confused and indecisive.

Ignited Dreams

Along the way many of us have let our dreams slip away, often in the name of a higher calling; a spouse, a child, extended family, obligations or work.

Day by day, piece by piece, our desires drift further away like the spent verdure of autumn trees shedding the very leaves that protected and nurtured them.

We allow the chaos of our days to erase the magic of our youthful hopes. What dreams we had then . . . promises that caused us to lose ourselves in reverie and doodle in the forgotten edges of childhood books.

When will we resurrect our smoldering desires and reignite the flames of passion that burned so bright?

Recapturing Our Youthful Spirits

When my world crumbled around me, for the umpteenth time—when I felt I could no longer pick up the pieces, or didn't want to try—I had an epiphany. I recalled my early passion; creating beauty from the forgotten and forlorn. It was then that I chose to recapture my giddy imaginings. I summoned up my warrior spirit, and shook the sleeping giant. And, that moment—that decision—changed how I directed and decorated my life.

> *Tossed and Turned . . . Decorating with the Thrift Diva* *takes you on an amazing journey—showing you how to surround yourself with the "real" you—tables, lamps, chairs and accents— all for a fraction of the normal cost. You will discover staging and decorating skills that you didn't know you had. And, you will have the time of your life.*

Visit America's "Thrift Talk" Diva, Barb Tobias

www.ThriftTalkDiva.com

About Barb Tobias

Before Barb Tobias ventured into the writing world she had no clue that her passion for thrift, her knack for decorating and a dire but reluctant need to practice frugality would turn her home from frumpy to fabulous and this enterprising woman into America's *Thrift Talk Diva.*

Her rich and diverse background has taken her from teacher, to fashion model to dog trainer to decorator. But it was her love for thrift and talent as a radio and television personality that led to the launch of Thrift Talk Diva, LLC providing the platform for her speaking, coaching and entertainment career.

Born and raised in the Midwest, Barb and her husband, now share their frugally elegant mountain home, nestled in the towering peaks and pines of the Rockies, with two Portuguese Water Dogs, a myriad of elk, and a scattering of bear and mountain lion.

Contact Barb Tobias at:

BarbTobias@ThriftTalkDiva.com
www.ThriftTalkDiva.com

Speaking Opportunities

Barb Tobias's rich and diverse experiences have transformed her from farm girl to fashion model to America's "Thrift Talk" Diva. However, it was her talent as a radio and TV personality that provided the platform for her speaking and coaching career.

Barb Tobias uses a proven, step-by-step system designed to help audiences achieve goals and dreams while having fun. Audiences receive decades of wisdom every time she speaks. Dynamic and knowledgeable, Barb warms the room with her keynotes, workshops, breakouts, conventions and associations, retreats, and spouse events.

The following programs can range from an hour keynote to an all day workshop:

Thrift
- How to Live Like Royalty on a Pauper's Budget
- The Frugal Fashionista
    Dressing for the Red Carpet … on Pennies

Motivation
- A Journey …
    From Farm Girl to Fashion Model to America's "Thrift Talk" Diva
- So You Missed the Boat; Buy Another Ticket
    Starting over when you're too old, too tired, too qualified and just too, too!

Decorating
- Decorating like A Diva
    … on a Pauper's Budget
- From Road-Kill to Road-Thrill
    …Living the Life of "RE

Business
- Smart Marketing … Big Payoffs
- The Entrepreneur … Unleashed!

Empowering Women
- Finding your *Diva-ness*
    …And flaunting it!

To Book Barb Tobias for Your Next Event:

1-877-771-DIVA (3482)
BarbTobias@ThriftTalkDiva.com

Coaching Opportunities

Barb has climbed up stiff peaks, visited murky valleys and has become the Diva of reinvention. During her lifelong quest toward self-discovery she learned how to capture the magic in the mundane. Today she shares her extraordinary abilities…

Believe in your MAGIC
- Learn How to Create a Remarkable, Fulfilling Life
- Boost Your Self-confidence

Recapture your ENERGY
- Surround Yourself with Positive Energy
- Achieve a Healthy Work-Life Balance

Feel your POWER
- Dream BIG; Live Passionately
- Turn Your Dreams into Reality

Get READY to . . .
- Break Through Self-limiting Beliefs
- Blast Away Procrastination
- Discover New Approaches to Old Ideas

What people are saying …

Barb Tobias, America's Thrift Talk Diva, is an inspiration! She was the speaker for Women, Wine, and Wellness in July 2010, and she was fantastic. Her presentation was polished, professional, interactive, entertaining, and her topic was well received and valuable to our group. I highly recommend hiring her for speaking engagements. She will exceed your expectations!

~ Lisa Shultz, Founder of Women, Wine and Wellness

To Book Barb Tobias:

1-877-771-DIVA (3482)
BarbTobias@ThriftTalkDiva.com

A Thrifty Order Form

To order the book or audio CD of *Tossed & Found* via U.S. Mail, please remove/copy this page and return the completed form to:

Thrift Talk Diva • P.O. Box 1077 • Evergreen, CO 80437
1-877-711-DIVA (3482) • www.ThriftTalkDiva.com

Send to (please print):

_____
Name

_____
Address

_____
City   State   Zip   Country

_____
Email

_____ Books - *Tossed & Found … Where Frugal is Chic* – Per copy: $20
U.S. Shipping & Handling – Per copy: $7
$20 each (U.S.) includes $7/copy shipping & handling
$1.50 S/H for each additional book   Books Subtotal: _____

_____ CDs - *Tossed & Found …Where Frugal is Chic*
(4 CD's; read by author) – Per set: $80
US Shipping & Handling – Per copy: $8
$88 each set (U.S.) includes $8/CD: shipping & handling
$2.50 S/H for each additional set   CDs Subtotal: _____

_____ Book/CD Package Special – *Tossed & Found* – Per set: $70
US Shipping & Handling – Per set: $10
$80 package includes $10 per item: shipping & handling
$5 S/H for each additional bundle   Book and CD Package Subtotal: _____

Total enclosed with order: _____

Please pay by check or money order, payable to: **Thrift Talk Diva**

Credit Card Method of Payment:
___Check ___Cash ___Credit Card (Visa, MC, Discover) # of copies: _____

Credit Card number _____   Exp Date: _____

CVV # (3 digits on back): _____

Shipping Address: _____

City, State, Zip: _____

Phone: _____ E-mail: _____

Street address #, Zip Code of billing address of card (if different):

_____

* Prices subject to change